OWN IT

OWN IT

Unlocking The Power of Influence

BRANDON LEE WHITE

This book is dedicated to my wife, Rachel, who helps me take ownership of what matters most: relationships.

I love you.

TABLE OF CONTENTS

PART 1 - You

PART 2 - More than You

Own It

/ōn/ /it/

verb phrase

1. To take responsibility for or go after something with passion and purpose.

FOREWORD

Have you ever wondered why some people have so much impact while others struggle to be heard? As an international professional speaker and trainer, I have had the privilege of working alongside Human Resources leaders across a vast spectrum of industries—from the military, government agencies, and food services to manufacturing, healthcare, and entertainment. These experiences have offered me unique insight into how some people develop more influence, build more positive relationships, and become better leaders. And one truth stands out: You have to start with yourself.

It is from this vantage point that I wholeheartedly endorse *Own It* by Brandon Lee White. This book is far more than a guide for self-improvement; it is a manual for leveling up at work, home, and within the community.

Within these pages, White delivers practical strategies and refreshing perspectives for anyone desiring to increase their influence through personal development. It is so applicable and powerful that I launched a training program based on what I learned from this book, which got rave reviews.

White's approach is both transformative and empowering. He demonstrates that by taking ownership of our attitudes, mentalities, actions, and issues (our Marks, Mosts, and Monsters) we not only improve ourselves, but create a ripple effect that elevates our relationships, strengthens our families and teams, and propels our organizations forward. In my career, I have seen firsthand how such ownership can unlock the door to authentic leadership—where trust, empathy, and genuine connection are the foundations of influence.

Own It empowers us to recognize the profound impact we have on others, and it challenges us to wield that influence with responsibility and purpose. As you read, you will discover tools for self-reflection, actionable ideas for personal growth, and inspiring stories that illuminate the journey from individual development to collective success.

Brandon Lee White invites us to truly own our influence and unlock our power. This book is your opportunity to embrace that challenge and to step confidently into your life role that shapes your family, friends, cultures, and industries. The rewards—improved relationships, greater influence, and lasting results—are well worth the commitment.

I invite you to turn these pages with an open mind and a willingness to act. Own your influence, lead with purpose, and watch as your impact multiplies—within yourself, your organization, and beyond. Now is your time! Own It!

— Kathy Bote'

INTRO

As of writing this book, I have presented to roughly one million people nationwide about taking ownership of their lives from the inside out. From a young age, I have witnessed people including my teachers, coaches, and employers having varying degrees of influence. I've had people coerce me toward action and others inspire me toward improvement. I've had people I liked and people I did not like. Was the difference their intellect? No. Was it their charisma? No. Was it their years of experience? No. The difference was something more powerful: intentional relationships. They took ownership of what I call the 3Cs: comfortable in themselves, confident in their abilities, and most importantly, caring toward me. These 3Cs, as we will discuss in the book, are the heart of relational influence. This book teaches you to be a more comfortable, confident, and caring person who can connect, resolve conflict, and lead.

Great influence with others starts with a great relationship within yourself. You must, first, have a healthy relationship with yourself before you can have healthy relationships with others. From the fertile soil of a healthy inner relationship, self-confidence, humility, ambition, and influence grows. You begin to like the person in the mirror, the goals of your future, and the friends in your life. You become proud of yourself, passionate about your pursuits, and connected meaningfully with others. You become someone whom others trust and aspire to emulate. You become someone who others want to follow.

Many people want to become relationally influencial but are unsure how to own it. I can relate. I can get fixed on myself; addicted to virtual praise, distracted with busy work, and stuck scrolling screens. I can let myself hold me back.

This book is about taking ownership of better relationships and becoming a relational leader. This book is not just for management. It's for all people, regardless of title, because everyone can influence others, and influence is leadership.

The "own it" mentality implies taking responsibility for what's yours: your opportunity to improve the world around you by how you respond to it. When you take ownership of what you have and what you can do with it, everyone benefits. This book creates clarity and develops skills to help you live a more authentic, fulfilling, and impactful life from the inside out.

This book is divided into two parts. Part One is about you: your relationship with yourself and owning who you are, flaws and all. It includes self-acceptance and self-improvement. You will identify the enemy within that is working against you and reclaim it from fear and doubt. You will build better attitudes and take ownership of what you want the most. Part Two is about more than you: learning various communication and other leadership skills, regardless of your title.

I want to laugh from the gut, love from the heart, live stories worth sharing, and influence people toward better places. Here's an invitation for you to join me in becoming a relational leader. Let's own it.

PART 1 - YOU

(Your Relationship with Yourself)

CHAPTER 1

OWN YOUR "MARKS"

~

"Own how you're made and make who you are."

- Brandon Lee White

I like white shoes. The moment I put them on, I transform into a walking 1982 Michael Jackson *Thriller* album. Pair them with a white sweater and light blue jeans. Good to go. I order a coffee and walk through town like a Macklemore music video, humming a vibe that all is right. Then, without warning, it happens. Maybe it's my fault. Maybe it's someone else's fault, but it happens. A stroke of clumsiness, or perhaps fate, seems inevitable. The white shoes receive their first mark. A single scuff sours the coffee, dampens the music, and ruins the vibe. I can sometimes scrub it out, but I'm fighting a losing battle. The truth is that white shoes get marks.

Try to avoid marks, scrub if you must, but live your

life. Own it. Marks on shoes are proof that you are living. "Markless" shoes are like unlit candles, unopened collectible toys, and vintage cars under tarps. They may not get scuffed up, but they're not being enjoyed. A better life has marks on it. Take the risks, take the trips, make the mistakes, learn the lessons, create the memories, and leave the impact.

OK, enough motivational speaker stuff. I'll be honest...

I'm scared of rejection.

I worry about what others think of me.

I can put on masks and try hard to be some perfect avatar version of myself. I want to hide my marks, which is normal, but dysfunctional inner relationships, unfortunately, are normal.

I can settle for predictable devices in isolation over purposeful adventures with others. Why? I'm scared of rejection. Why am I scared of rejection? Sometimes, I don't think I'm "enough."

We must start with our mentality. If you think you're not enough, you won't give yourself enough to succeed. You won't give yourself enough second chances, encouragement, or hope. You give yourself what you need so that you can be what others need: a supporter, an accountability partner, and a role model.

We are hungry for happiness. In silent desperation, we grasp for happiness in technology, pleasure, achievements, and status all while avoiding the inner person who desires those things. It's as if the thing we want the most scares us the most. What is that thing we want the most? Although this "thing" creates happiness, it's deeper than happiness; it's connection. A connection is a mutual understanding, acceptance, and encouragement between two people. Yet, can't we be disconnected from ourselves? Do we talk to ourselves? Yes, because we have a relationship with ourselves, but not always a healthy one. Our negativity and unhealthy self-talk pushes us away from growth and toward self-consumption.

A healthy connection with yourself includes being honest about what you feel and being able to see the meaningful desires behind the shallow habits of fear and pleasure. We must start on the inside to build something better on the outside. We must own who we are, flaws and all, before we can become the relational influencers we're meant to be.

BAD MENTALITY: "I'M NOT ENOUGH"

Too many people are unhappy because they think they're not enough. They believe their "marks" equal their worth. True happiness comes from being able to make peace with your imperfections. You cannot seek perfection and have peace of mind at the same time. You'll end up jealous and bitter.

We're all critical of different things. Some people are more critical of their appearance, while others are more critical of their performance. Perfection doesn't exist, and you can't find or obtain something that doesn't exist. You will never be happy if you set unrealistic expectations for yourself. Appreciate what is. There is room for, and even a need for, improvement, but improvement for what can be will not bring additional happiness if you can't enjoy the improvement already made.

We are imperfect. Own it. Own your "marks."

OUTER MARKS

Most people are thinking the same thing every day, "How do I look?" Do you think you're too short, tall, thin, or fat? Do you despise your hair, nose, eyes, lips, skin, feet, stomach, booty, or freckles? You see your undesirable features as marks on a shoe that can't be scrubbed off. Maybe you try to cover them or enhance them, but often, you're stuck with them.

I've never liked my big ears and pointy nose. Well, at least I see them that way. Plus, I'm getting older, and that "dad bod" is constantly wanting to introduce itself to the world. How about some thinning hair to add to the cart? Yay.

I've always had a love-hate relationship with my body. I wasn't a great swimmer growing up because I didn't want to go to the pool and take my shirt off for fear of being made fun of for being overweight. It was the same story in basketball practice when we had to take our shirts off. People would tease me and say things like, "You have bigger boobies than your girlfriend!" Yeah... emotional damage.

Fast forward to when I was in high school/college and became skinny. I saw guys get muscular. Meanwhile, I stayed slender. Even my brother and father were taller and more muscular than I was. I thought I wasn't a man unless I had either height or muscles. Look at any popular action movie, for crying out loud! Imagine a skinny Thor during that scene where the shirt blows off in *Thor: God of Thunder*. It wouldn't be a scene! Once, I was insecure about being overweight. Now, I was insecure about being skinny. Did you know that Spider-Man is 5' 10" and 167 pounds? The truth that I needed to own was that I wasn't Thor. I was Spider-Man. Well... you know what I mean.

Nothing was wrong with me being 165 pounds. I simply didn't want my two little boys to wonder, "Who would win a wrestling match against Daddy and Mommy?" Not in my house! Mommy is surprisingly strong, by the way. So, I put in the work with weightlifting, and now I'm around 185 pounds, and Mommy doesn't stand a chance!

Body image is a complex thing. Some people hide behind the phrase, "Love your body," and use it to neglect their body by overeating and under-exercising. Others say, "Perfect your body," which is also harmful, not to mention impossible. There is a balance between accepting yourself and improving yourself.

There is a scene in *Avengers: End Game* in which Dr. Strange meditates on the millions of possibilities to defeat Thanos. He convulses as his brain calculates at AI speed. Suddenly, he stops and looks at Iron Man with a sober realization that there is only one path worth taking for success. Little did Iron Man know that the path Dr. Strange saw was one in which Iron Man sacrificed himself for the greater good.

As I stared at my ears in the mirror and powdered my hair with some thickening product, I saw what Dr. Strange saw. I knew the only path worth taking was one where I changed my mentality, sacrificed my stupid ego, and owned it. I can scrub a little, but the tarp must come off the '67 Corvette, and the candles must burn a glorious unapologetic flame with "This is Me" from *The Greatest Showman* playing in the background. Gosh, I love that movie.

> **"If you think you're not enough, you won't give yourself enough to succeed."**

Let me tell you something that many of us don't realize. Yes, there is a standard of beauty that almost everyone recognizes, such as the standard in magazines and models. Still, people forget that attraction is much more than physical appearance. People are attracted to, platonically and romantically, people who are comfortable, confident, and caring toward others.

I dated a girl in college who would not be considered physically attractive by common standards. But I was into this girl. There was something about her. She was comfortable and confident in herself. She had a warm and fun energy that was both calming and exciting. She was caring but not clingy. She seemed to know who she was, not pretending to be perfect and not ashamed of her imperfections. Many people didn't understand why I liked her, but I did. Attraction is more than looks. When you stop living insecurely, start owning who you are, and focus on others, you *are* more attractive.

It's funny and sad how we falsely think people care more about the shape of our noses than how fun we are to be around or how kind we are. Seriously, it doesn't matter if you're good-looking if people think you're stuck up, boring, or mean. In the movie *I Feel Pretty*, Amy Schumer plays an insecure woman who suddenly wakes up thinking she is beautiful, but her outside appearance hasn't changed. She goes from timidly apologetic to confidently unapologetic because her mind tricked her into believing she was beautiful when looking in the mirror. After months of thinking she was beautiful, she suddenly realized none of it was real. She was who she was. Her appearance never changed. Yet, during that time, she made friends, took risks, and advanced her career based on her false confidence. She realized that her life improved, not because of her appearance, but because of how she presented herself to others.

So, scrub a little if you want. Use some makeup and filters. There's nothing wrong with shining the exterior, but realize that the engine is more important than the paint job. Own how you're made, but more importantly, make who you are. Don't let your looks be the best thing about you. When a friend sees you, let them think, "I'm glad you are my friend because you're a good person who makes me smile."

Don't let them think, "I'm glad you're my friend because you have a pretty face or big muscles."

Respect your body and make it presentable, but let your confidence come from a source of inner strength, not outer facades. Inspire others to let go and be themselves. Give people the courage to smile from the inside out.

INNER MARKS

Inner marks are the emotional damage you wish you could erase. They can't be seen on the body, but they weigh heavily on the heart and mind. They are the disappointments, embarrassments, mistakes and sadness scuffed onto your heart by yourself and others. They mark up your spirit and threaten to turn you into a jaded, cold-hearted person.

Inner marks are like bad songs on repeat, causing depression and anxiety. Trauma from seeing your parents fight, experiencing the death of a loved one, moving away from friends, having nasty rumors spread about you, being stabbed in the back by a close friend, bullying, sexual abuse, being dumped by someone you loved, and so many other possible heart-breaking scenarios make it easy to see how people can lose their spark as they grow older.

Overall, I've lived a very good life so far. Many people have had worse inner marks than me. I can't complain too much. Still, I can raise my hand to say that I have experienced all those inner marks listed above. Those things hurt me. Without proper healing, they worsen like a cut on a leg that becomes infected from neglect.

I know from experience that our emotions can break like an arm. Unlike a bone, which requires medical attention and time to heal, we don't always pay attention to the things that break in our heads and hearts. There isn't a quick fix like putting on a cast, taking painkillers, and watching TV until it heals. Instead, we often replay the guilt and the hurt so often that it ceases to be useful. Nothing is being processed, learned from, or improved upon. It's only being slowly consumed like a homemade poison.

I don't want people to experience emotional pain, but I also know it's impossible to live in a bubble. Life equals marks. The goal is not to avoid pain but to learn how to recycle it into something better. Pain can be useful. Pain teaches. Pain develops grit. Pain connects people as it provides opportunities for compassion and love. Pain motivates people to make necessary changes.

Imagine if humans invented a way to take their trash and put it in a processor that converts it to batteries to power anything in their homes or vehicles. We would never run out of energy. That's how I think of pain. Like trash, pain is a byproduct of life. What if we processed pain in a way that actually helped us?

THE MENTALITY FOR MARKS

The mentality for marks is that marks happen; own them and use them for good. Taking ownership doesn't mean you must do everything on your own. It means you must take the first step in helping yourself, even if that means asking for help. No one can help you if you're not ready to help yourself. They're your marks, not someone else's. Whether it's a mistake you need to learn from and make the best of, or if it's something that unfairly happens to you, own it. Take responsibility for what needs to happen next. Process your feelings and grow from your marks.

1. CHANGE YOUR PERSPECTIVE

Step one in growing through your marks is to be able to change your perspective and see marks differently. I was at a church camp watching a painter on stage. With a paintbrush in hand, he looked at the massive blank canvas resting on an easel. I watched curiously as he began attacking the canvas with broad, unruly strokes of colors. Like a wild Beethoven, he composed art through his fingertips. Everything he painted was abstract. It made no sense. Lines, blotches, and swirls danced with no order, no meaning.

"What's the point of this?" I thought judgmentally. But before I could say more, the painter paused. He slowly stepped back from his painting, carefully grabbed the still-wet artwork, and turned it upside down. I let out a breath of realization as a beautiful image of Jesus wearing a crown of thorns came into focus. I thought it was pointless, but I just had the wrong perspective. It's not pointless, it's beautiful.

Let's flip the common belief that you must be "markless" to be liked. I'll prove it. Do you like your grandparents because they look like supermodels? Yeah, that's weird. Of course not. Shout out to my grandpa, who, by the way, is a good-looking dude. Anyway, my point is people don't truly like other people for how they look or because they seem perfect and never make mistakes. Actually, people can be disliked for seeming too "perfect" because they're unrelatable, and they can make others feel bad about themselves. My point is that perfection doesn't make people like you. People like you because you embrace their imperfections. That's love.

2. BE HEARD TO BE HEALED

With the right perspective, we can process our marks and heal our pain. Processing marks include sharing feelings and being heard. I will unapologetically grab the microphone and proclaim that our culture needs to get better at talking about feelings. Talking about feelings doesn't make you weak; being unwilling to talk about them does.

Talk about inner marks with someone who cares. Get the feelings out in the air where they can no longer grow mold in the dark. If you don't process feelings and recycle their toxic waste, mental illness grows like algae on a stagnant pond. Talking about it and feeling understood flushes it out. The empathy felt by someone listening to you can heal wounds or at least begin the process. I understand finding someone who will listen and empathize well can be hard.

In the movie Inside Out, the character Sadness brought Riley happiness through listening. She didn't try to fix Riley; she simply listened with empathy. Listening with empathy means trying to feel what the other person feels. The character Joy tried so hard to make Riley happy by forcing happiness, but Joy was afraid to allow the pain in. Inner marks must be heard to be healed before someone can be happy again. Don't make the mistake that many do of trying to "sweep it under the rug." Allowing yourself to process the sadness brings back joy. Let me say that again. You must process the sadness to reclaim the joy. Try it. Talk with someone, anyone you trust. Start to heal your inner marks.

BASKETBALL BLUES

I used to be hung up on how my high school basketball career ended poorly because of an injury. This nagged at me and even caused recurring dreams as an adult. In my dreams, I was back in my Senior year, desperately trying to succeed but always falling

*short. I played pickup games at YMCAs after high
school and tried reliving the glory days.*

*I shared my feelings with my wife even though I felt
embarrassed. I mean, come on, get over it, man.
It's just a game! But to me, it was more. It was my
childhood dream. It was unfinished work that began
when I was five in my backyard, shooting hoops.
It was a coach who I felt never genuinely believed
in me and who I thought I let down. I sought his
approval like a pseudo-father but was left feeling
estranged.*

*Talking with my wife and thinking it through
helped me see what I didn't see. I realized that part
of my inner mark was correlated to my relationship
with my biological father, whom I sought to gain
approval from. As my relationship with him
improved, it helped my basketball blues.*

*I gained another perspective when I stepped back
and talked about it. I realized that I thought I was
better than I actually was. I scolded myself for never
making 20 points in a game. The truth is that even
with unlimited practice, my potential had a limit.
Given my size and talent, I could be good, but not
as great as I wanted. The truth is that I should have
practiced more in high school, but the truth is that
I also wasn't meant to be a professional basketball*

player. When I accepted this, I was finally able to move on.

I no longer have basketball dreams, and my memory of high school basketball has changed. I don't see it as a huge disappointment. I see it as a sport I played pretty well and had a handful of good memories, such as hitting a couple of game-winning shots. It wasn't meant to be my all. It was meant to be an experience to build from. Being heard and changing my perspective helped me heal.

One of the worst things someone can do with an inner mark is nothing. A negative loop is created when people pause their lives because they're replaying bad past events. Sort out your feelings and free the negative hold they have on you. Be heard because you matter. Be healed because you have a life worth living.

3. HUMOR DEPOWERS MARKS

Humor empowers people not to take themselves too seriously and to take back the power that "marks" steal. I can make an excellent monkey impression that makes kids laugh on command when I pull my ears and puff out my cheeks. Last Christmas, my little nephew innocently said, "You look like an elf with your pointy nose and ears." I laughed out loud because he wasn't trying to be mean. He was just being honest. I could have gotten offended and said, "That's not nice!" Instead, I swallowed a humility pill and laughed with him about myself. A sign of emotional maturity is the ability to laugh at yourself and life's letdowns in a healthy way.

I know that some inner marks aren't funny, such as

> "Perfection doesn't make people like you. People like you because you embrace their imperfections."

abuse, but there are other things you can laugh about, such as embarrassing moments. For example, I had a buddy who was in church and telling a story on stage about camping. He meant to say, "Pitch my tent," about camping. Instead, he accidentally said, "Pinch my tits." Yeah…not even kidding. He was humiliated, some were offended, and others, like me, were wildly amused. He felt terrible then, but now it's his favorite funny story to tell.

Outer and inner marks require the same remedy: "Own it." If you don't own your marks, they will own you. They'll own your thoughts, which turn into your actions, which turn into your future.

Accept the fact that the real world is messy and full of flaws. Have the mentality that "marks happen." True, you may be a bit of a mess now, aren't we all? But that mess is being molded. You're a work in progress, a rocky foundation that something amazing is being built.

You are worthy of love and needed by others. Grab

your painting and turn it upside down. Turn your marks into meaning and your pain into purpose. Balance between self-acceptance and self-improvement. Look in that mirror tonight and be a friend to yourself. Own what you've been given, own up to what you've done, and, as discussed in the next chapter, own what you want to do with it.

CHAPTER APPLICATION:

Own Your "Marks"

1. Do you struggle with the "I'm Not Enough" mentality? If so, how?

2. What are some of your "outer marks"? How can you see them from a more positive perspective?

3. What are some of your "inner marks"? How can you see them from a more positive perspective?

4. Who can you process your "inner marks" with?

5. Pick one "mark" and find the humor in it.

CHAPTER 2
Own Your "Mosts"

~

"Settling too much in life leads to an unsettled life."

- Brandon Lee White

There is something all people have in common: They want to have a good life. They all want to like the person in the mirror, the goals of their future, and the friends in their lives. They want to be proud of themselves, passionate about their activities, and meaningfully connected with others. This is what everyone wants. This is what you want the *most*.

"MOSTS" VS "NOWS"

"Mosts" are the things that matter most to you. "Nows" are lesser things you settle for in moments of impatience. "Nows" are fueled by feelings that don't have your best interests in mind. For example, when I feel insecure in the "now" moment, I want to hide from people or put on a mask they'll approve of. When I feel angry in the "now" moment, I want to get revenge or shut down and distance myself. When I feel tempted in the "now" moment, I want to give into my cravings and sabotage my larger goals. The "now" feels loud and urgent, so I want to settle and submit to its barking orders and bullying behavior. The problem is that it rarely is the best option as it often takes more than it gives.

"Mosts" call out to you, encouraging you not to settle but instead to go for it. They speak wisdom and point a steady finger toward a better future. These include your vocational and personal passions. Are you connected to your passions and the talents that those passions reveal? "Mosts" are your big dreams, bold passions, and deep relationships. We must prioritize our "mosts" above our "nows." The problem is that the same fear surrounding your "marks" surrounds your "mosts."

PURSUING MY "MOST"

I remember when I was ten. I knew I was going to be the next Michael Jordan. I believed it. I believed in myself. By age 15, I didn't believe that anymore. By age 20, I let go of my second dream of being an actor. My world appeared flatter each year as life seemed to seep through the plastic cap. Suddenly, instead of chasing dreams, I was swiping screens.

I was 22 and in college, earning a Master's in Business, but I was unsure if I wanted to work in the corporate world. I thought I should leave my childhood dreams behind and focus on a realistic job. One day, my father reminded me of my passion for working with young people and how I could make a living as a motivational speaker for students. I could still use my love for acting and other hobbies, such as dancing while speaking on stage. My almost-completed master's degree could be used for self-employment.

Still, I needed to invest. I needed to take a risk because all great adventures require risk. I found a virtual training program to teach me how to be a motivational youth speaker. The cost was $1000. That was a lot of money for me. Immediately, I became nervous about failing and losing my money. What if I'm not good enough? It would be just another dream that stayed a dream. I wanted to retreat to the predictable path of streaming shows and "safe degrees," but something inside me knew I was meant for something else. Would I follow in the footsteps of the many or lead a path worth following?

It was time to own my "mosts." I wanted to be a professional motivational speaker who helps people live better lives. I wanted my "mosts," but it wasn't enough to want them. I needed to train and prepare for them. The ancient Greek poet Archilochus said, "We don't rise to the level of our expectations; we fall to the level of our training." I spent the $1000 for the training and completed every lesson: created my message, built my website, made a promo video, and marketed it to schools and conferences. There weren't always absolute answers. I had to decide on my content, design, and so on. I had to take leaps of faith without an adult or parent telling me exactly what to do or how to do it.

I felt alive inside and aligned with my calling as my imagination placed me on stage, bringing students to laughter, wonder, and the edge of tears. My tech-dopamine addiction lessened as my passion and purpose strengthened. I had less boredom because I was living in my "mosts."

On the day of my first paid speech, I was flooded with nerves and felt a case of imposter syndrome. I owned it. I faced it. I made it. My speech was a success, but it was far from perfect. Looking back, I cringe and chuckle at how far I've come. Now, I'm a leading youth speaker in The United States. I've written several books, started a nonprofit, hosted conferences, and helped others become speakers. My job can still be difficult, but I love it. I feel fulfilled

*and blessed because I'm living out what I'm meant
to do: working for myself as a motivational speaker
and professional writer.*

"Mosts" always include meaningful relationships with people. My "mosts" included a big dream to help people all around the country through my speeches and books to take ownership of their lives. It wouldn't have been a great "most" if I had spent all that time speaking in front of a mirror.

An even greater "most" than my career is my desire to be a good husband and father and be close to God. What kind of a relational leader would I be if I was positively influencing people through my books and speeches but neglecting my own wife and kids? Unfortunately, this seems to be a common habit among many of us. We try to win over people who aren't as close to us because shallow acceptance is easier than deep connection.

The key ingredient of a "most" is relationship. Many people withhold the essential relational component and poison their "mosts." Their careers, hobbies, and households become self-centered islands in the desert, dehydrated of authentic personal connection and meaningful impact. The mirage appears successful, but the reality is much more depressing. The marriage, the relationships with the kids, the relationships, or lack thereof, with friends and coworkers all suffer, leaving people scratching for satisfaction in their trivial pursuits.

I'll be honest, I love golf, but it can easily become unhealthy for me because it becomes destructively self-serving and self-focused. My goal is to get better so that I can feel better about myself, and if I'm honest, impress others. I'm not influencing others much through golf. It can easily become an egocentric activity for me. This doesn't mean I'm going to quit golf, but I need to learn to shift my mentality away from myself and move it more toward the people I golf with. That's it. It's about the relationships. Your "mosts" are not about impressing others through achievements, shying away from others through screens, or fooling others with false versions of yourself. "Mosts" are the meaningful desires that bring out the best in you so that you can bring out the best in others.

The joy and impact of "mosts" exists in the quality of the relational influence, not just the functional improvement. Many managers seek functional improvement without relational influence. This includes improving bottom line results without connecting with the hearts of the people, who are the engines of the company. Sure, it's not all hugging and singing songs. Leadership includes accountability and even boundaries, but it's the relationships and the relational skills that are the horses that pull the carts. Before we put all blame on management, each employee has a responsibility to take personal ownership of being the change they want to see. That's why we are first focusing on our inner relationships, because we won't have healthy relationships with others until we have healthy relationships with ourselves.

NOT SETTLING

Most of us start genuinely optimistic about the "mosts" of our future, but our fears convince us to settle. We settle with distractions to cope with anxiety and disappointments. Here's the truth: Distraction is the easiest way to dull a dissatisfied life without fixing it. Cheap entertainment doesn't equal deep fulfillment. I'm guilty. While writing this book, I often escaped to social media for a quick dopamine hit to offset my fear. Taking a break is fine, but when the break becomes a way of living, we're no longer truly living. We get antsy about the stresses and boredom of life, and so, like an addict, we seek relief, a little scratch for the itch, usually in the form of a rectangle in our hands. That's not the life we're meant to live.

It's scary to make goals, connect with people, apologize, forgive, or ask for help. On the other hand, it's scary to imagine a boring life where you're constantly settling for less than what you were meant for. Scary is growing old without feeling you've truly lived a meaningful relationship with yourself and others.

The problem is that we want better lives but tend to settle for lamer ones. Instead of building character, we build high scores on addictive phone games. We prioritize draining entertainment over true fulfillment. Why? We settle for safer and easier.

Abraham Lincoln said, "Discipline is choosing what you want the most over what you want now." That's the secret to a better life. Instead, a lack of discipline allows FOMO, "fear of missing out," to trade better things in the future for pressing things in the present.

Don't fall into the trap of caring more about your current feelings than your future well-being. Go after what matters to you the most. Sure, I believe in living wisely, not recklessly. But there is a fine line when playing it too safe becomes more reckless than wise. I hear elderly people say that their biggest regrets aren't the things they did and failed but the things they didn't do, and now it's too late to try.

> **"There is a fine line when playing it too safe becomes more reckless than wise."**

If I scrolled through the pictures on your phone, are they filled with proud moments? Are they filled with "mosts?" If you start settling for a life you don't want, don't complain when you're unhappy. Settling too much in life leads to an unsettled life. Ironically, settling to avoid discomfort just creates different kinds of discomfort: boredom, misaligned careers, missed opportunities, and regret.

If you feel bored, lost, and aimlessly floating through life, you're not living out your "mosts" in a relational way. You're not clear about what you want, you're not connected to yourself and others, and you're not actively pursuing those things. I give you no guilt trip. I give you permission to ask yourself, "What do I want the most for and from my life?"

BAD MENTALITY: "I CAN'T"

The "I Can't" mentality is the enemy of "mosts." It makes slimy deals with "now" feelings. Its negativity, rooted in fear, settles for weak moves and lame moments. This mentality keeps us from having hard conversations and taking big adventures because it convinces us to give up before we get started. As a result, we don't take the road less traveled into the great unknown. We don't find the true freedom that lies past our fears and discomforts. We don't connect with the people around us.

Some have a risk-averse personality. Others lack role models and leaders to encourage them to take positive actions. Some experience failure and embarrassing moments that shy them away from believing in themselves and trying again. Still, some might truly believe they "can't" because of low self-esteem, but often, it's a matter of "I won't." Laziness is a smooth talker and a robber of joy. I've been enticed by its crafty lies, such as, "It's not worth it. It probably won't work. Maybe next week. Don't worry about it. It's too hard."

How does this play out in people's futures? It looks nothing like their childhood dreams. They settle for jobs that fail to utilize their passions and talents to their fullest. Their focus becomes to get a check to make ends meet. I'm not talking about people who have misfortunes. I'm talking about people who choose to settle for undesirable lives because they're afraid or lazy. They settle for dysfunctional relationships because they don't want to work to improve them, assuming they can be improved. They settle for addictions because they are afraid to ask for help. I'm not ridiculing people with addictions. I know addiction can be a disease and very hard to overcome. I'm saying that it's not someone's fault if they have an addiction, but it begins to become their fault when they don't take ownership and seek help. It's about not settling.

I get it. It's not always that simple. Life costs more each year, especially if you choose to have kids. Sometimes, we must compromise our passions for careers that, although not ideal, pay the bills. If that's the case, don't throw away your passions. Make them hobbies and areas of service. Include what truly matters to you in your life. For example, a friend of mine has a hobby of woodworking. So, he made wooden animals for kids at the church. Another friend never became a singer, but he does monthly karaoke with friends. Keep your passions in your life even if they're not your career. Use those passions to connect with others. Passion is powerful and inspirational.

CHARACTER MAKES "MOSTS" POSSIBLE

Character is what makes "mosts" possible. It is the proper foundation of your life, and it helps you overcome fear and laziness. It helps you focus on sharing love with others rather than storing up pleasure for yourself. Character brings out the best in you while protecting you from the worst in you. Character is everything you want in a friend: kindness, responsibility, trustworthiness, perseverance, honesty, etc. Like a tree, the roots of character support your growth in life and protect you from storms like peer pressure, destructive habits, and misfortunes.

Character can't be streamed, bought, or stolen. You can't access it with a click of a button. You must develop it over time. People lacking character endanger themselves and those around them. They sacrifice what's truly important (mosts) for what's deceivingly urgent (nows). They choose comfort over character. They choose popularity over character. They choose fear over character.

The United States' biggest threat to a successful future isn't an external threat such as a foreign country; it's an internal threat: us. The best way to protect and preserve our freedom is to be self-governed from within and lead with character. The greater our goodness is within, the greater our ability to preserve goodness. When we model behavior and foster environments centered on wisdom, courage, discipline, and kindness, there is a hopeful future.

Our potential for growth or destruction is proportionate to our level of technology in relation to our morality. Consider the fantastic things humanity could accomplish through AI, but watch any action movie and see how advanced technology becomes an advanced weapon in the hands of those who lack humanity. We must advance our inner character as we develop outer technologies.

How do you build character? Expose yourself to people of character. Who do you know with qualities that you admire? Talk to them, invite them to lunch, and, I know it sounds crazy, become their friend. We can't help but be influenced by the people we associate with. Simultaneously, limit or remove the things and influences that weaken your character, such as certain media and people. You can't have a clean house if you keep letting dogs track their dirty paws inside. I've seen people start wholesome but darken in their character as they were exposed to unwholesome movies, books, music, and people. Trash in, trash out.

You must practice character to improve character. We all know those moments, those little tests, that give us a chance to practice character. Instead of being paralyzed with fear of the big war, focus on winning little battles in the moment. You don't have to win every battle, but the more little battles you win, the more your character grows. Do it to be it.

IF YOUR LIFE WERE A MOVIE

Imagine your life is a big movie, and you're the main character. As the director, pause your life and say, "Cut!" Step out of your body and look back at yourself. Look at yourself as the main character in a movie. You know this character's story, their strengths, weaknesses, and frustrations. From the outside looking in, what do you want for this character, and what do you want from this character? It's easy to know what you want for yourself: happiness, adventure, and peace of mind, but what do you want *from* yourself? Do you want to be more courageous, compassionate, patient, or disciplined? Make changes now in your movie before it's too late.

You are a beautiful, amazing person when you allow yourself to be. Don't settle for a lesser version of yourself. Own your "marks" and "mosts." Find your passions, rise with preparation, and live a better life. You won't live forever. You will get older, and opportunities will pass you by. Moments will be stuck in the past. It's time to own it. While others are wasting time, you're taking time. You're taking time to think of who you are and who you want to be. You're owning it, and I'm darn proud of you.

CHAPTER APPLICATION:

Own Your "Mosts"

1. Who and what are your "mosts," and why?

2. What distracts you from your "mosts," and how can you limit those distractions?

3. Do you struggle with the "I Can't" mentality? If so, how?

4. Give yourself an honest score on your character. Who and what can you add or remove to improve it?

5. If you were the director of your "life movie," what would you want your character to do more or less of? What would you want for and from yourself?

CHAPTER 3

OWN YOUR "MONSTERS"

~

"It's me, hi. I'm the problem; it's me."

-Taylor Swift

CAUGHT IN A LIE

I dated a girl when I was younger. Her tall, athletic frame complemented her strong spirit. She liked me. Unfortunately for her, I wasn't who she thought I was. I was someone whose core was infected with pride and discontent. Secretly, inside, I thought that I could do better. My mentality was, "She's good enough for now." Ironically, my chronic discontent with myself transformed into discontent with others. I wasn't good enough for myself, but neither were my girlfriends. Later in life, I would feel the bitter taste of my own medicine as a girl would dump me like a load of unwanted clothes at the thrift shop. It's not so much the breakup that crushes you but the feeling that the other person was playing you the whole time. You were falling hopelessly in love while also falling for a cruel realization that she was never that into you.

I knew the relationship wouldn't last, but I was too selfish and cowardly to cut it off before it grew legs. My girlfriend must have sensed my lack of loyalty. One night, I received a phone call from her friend. Her friend was pretty. I couldn't say much more about her because, honestly, that's mostly what I cared about back then.

"Hey, Brandon…" her voice was soft and inviting. "I know you're dating my friend, but I've always had feelings for you." I leaned into the phone with intrigue. "Do you think you and I could go out on a date? Your girlfriend doesn't have to know."

It felt good being pursued. I quickly weighed my options, like holding up two tomatoes in the grocery store to see which was more appealing. "Ok, sure," I said stupidly.

Suddenly, a familiar voice joined the conversation.

'We're done, Brandon." My girlfriend was listening

the whole time. The red tomatoes smashed against my face, and the embarrassment dripped onto the floor. Worse, I got mad and accused her of tricking me, which she did, but I deserved it. My true colors splattered all over me as my arrogance put on a pitiful display of classic defensiveness. That was a bad moment.

Lies are like boomerangs. They look good going out but come back to smack you in the face. When they hung up, I saw the boomerang upside down on the floor and felt the swelling mark it left behind. My mind raced like the fan blades above my head. It was a sharp lesson about honesty that, unfortunately, would take me several more years to learn.

I scuffed up that relationship as well as my integrity. At that moment, I didn't own my actions. I blamed the girls for tricking me, and I tried to pretend I wasn't humiliated. I was a "Schemer" who turned into a "Complainer," "Blamer," and "Exploder." It was an egotistical, disrespectful thing I did to my girlfriend. I was about to cheat on her with her best friend! I deserved to fall for that prank.

Your scariest monsters in life won't come from under your bed; they'll come from within. We are the problem. Raised on an unhealthy ego, "Me-Monsters" seek to sabotage their hosts by exploiting "marks" and undermining "mosts." They complain, "I can't be happy until I look a certain way, have so many followers, or win so many trophies." They mop ingly say, "I can't. It's not worth it. I'll just crawl into a hole and hate life." They arrogantly boast, "I'm better than others, and I deserve more."

They are reckless creatures that make messes and find someone else to blame. Instead of working hard and making better decisions, they say, "It's not my responsibility. It's not my fault. I just need a better job, family, etc." They're self-absorbed but not self-aware enough to make positive changes. They're driven by "now" feelings. They throw tantrums and will even hurt others, physically or emotionally, because they lack self-control. The sooner you take ownership of the monsters within you, the sooner you can go full Ghostbusters on them and be more of the better you. Developing this "better you" is the key to unlocking your influence.

Me-Monsters

THE EXPLODER: Short tempered, easily offended, defensive, lacks self-control and empathy, and explodes when they don't get their way or when disrespected.

THE COMPLAINER: Negative, avoids responsibility, can be lazy, entitled, self-centered, and complains when things get difficult. They aren't interested much in helping or providing solutions.

THE SCHEMER: Witty, manipulative, dishonest, deceiving, schemes for personal gain, and spreads rumors.

THE PEOPLE-PLEASER: Demonstrates an unhealthy desire to be liked and sacrifices personal convictions and authenticity for approval. They succumb to negative peer pressure and group think.

THE BRAGGER: Cares most about their own achievements and good qualities. They are self-absorbed with hidden insecurities. They are often not good at listening or encouraging others.

THE DISTANCER: Retreats into their thoughts and feelings while pushing others away. They disengage from contributing and experience an increase in self-pity or anger.

THE BLAMER: Points the blame and looks to punish rather than take accountability and encourage. They have negative mindsets and often lack trust.

THE EGO AND THE BAD WOLF

"Me-Monsters" originate from an unhealthy ego. The unhealthy ego magnifies the self and becomes the jailkeeper of your inner and outer marks. This gluttonous monster wants to gaze into the mirror a little too long, looking at what it likes and thinks it needs to be perfect. It wants to time travel and go back to change the past or control the future. The ego can keep you enslaved to a mentality of self-perfection and self-pity, which leads to self-destruction.

The paradox is that the self is better off, not by being more selfish but less selfish. Of course, the ego tries to hang on like a toddler in a Wal-Mart's toy aisle. As the adult within yourself, you can have the wisdom to realize that less of a selfish "me" is better because it allows the better "me" to develop.

There is a story of a wise Indian man who tells a young boy that inside all of us is a good wolf and a bad wolf. The wolves are constantly fighting and trying to kill each other. Wide-eyed, the young boy nervously asks, "Which one wins?" The wise Indian man answers, "The one you feed."

The bad wolf is another metaphor for the unhealthy ego. The ego is fed when you put yourself into the spotlight. You puff yourself up with your outer appearance or achievements, separating you from the "lowly common folk." This may give you a feeling of significance but only at the expense of connection. You can't feel better than everyone without losing connection with them.

The opposite is true when you're so insecure about your

imperfections that you shy away and think you're not good enough for connection. An unhealthy ego is not always arrogance. It's simply putting too much focus on the "self." The bad wolf tricks you into thinking you would be perfect, and people would like you if you could only scrub off your marks.

Clothes, cars, makeup, tattoos, money, apps, or even AI can't fill the void within that comes from a disconnect from yourself. When you create phony versions of yourself, you begin to glitch on the inside. The prison walls grow taller when you feed your ego with things like fear and selfishness. Instead, if you feed the good wolf love, humility, and encouragement, your freedom grows, and so does your happiness and positive impact on this world.

I'm not perfect. I foolishly slip snacks to the bad wolf daily. I scroll screens a bit too long, dwell on past events too much, and do things I know I shouldn't. I catch myself and continuously turn my attention back to the good wolf. That's owning it. Call out your self-destructive ways and turn back to the better you. You can be a bad person. We all can. But you can also be a good person. It's within you.

"Your scariest monsters in life won't come from under your bed; they'll come from within."

MY "ME-MONSTERS"

I seemed confident on the outside, but the real me was insecure on the inside. I was a "Bragger" at times, but I was also a "People-Pleaser" who wanted to change himself to make others like him. I could also be a "Distancer" and shut down when I felt discouraged or lost in my identity. My monsters kept saying, "If only I had a viral video. If only I had more followers. If only I had plastic surgery. If only I had more money...then I would be enough, enough to be loved and be happy." I wasn't brave enough to be myself. I remember knowing nice students whom I might have been good friends with, and I was nice to them at school, but I didn't hang out with them after school. I wanted to be with the popular crowd.

I did become popular. My good looks, talents, and social skills took me all the way to school president, homecoming king, drum major, and varsity captain. I had the parties on weekends and the ego to go with it. My thinking was wrapped up in status, and I developed an inflated view of myself.

I went to college, and my addiction to popularity grew. I became a small-time actor and model as a side job, which was fun, but it was also dog treats for my vanity. I was featured on various billboards and commercials, and the minor celebrity attention was pure cocaine to my ego.

I started my own t-shirt company with a friend. We had fashion shows and raised some money for some good causes.

Don't get me wrong, I was a nice guy and did a lot of good things, but underneath was an ego monster with its tentacles in every move I made.

When I watched The Greatest Showman, I saw a lot of my old self in the character P.T. Barnum. There is a strange connection between narcissism and discontent. On one hand, the arrogant person thinks they're all that, but on the other hand, they're deeply insecure, thinking they're not enough. They feel that they need to puff up the outside for what is lacking on the inside. The outward approval they seek is simply a second-rate version of the inward acceptance they need.

The song "Never Enough" in the movie convicted me of my tendency to be chronically discontent with myself. I wanted to live out an ideal image. The wretched beast within me hunted for personal glorification. It hungered for the praise but never found its fill.

At the end of the movie, P.T. Barnum learned what truly matters: relationships. He watched his daughter perform a small role in a school play, and while sitting in the audience, he sang the same lyrics from his once big-time show, but with a different meaning this time. "It's everything you ever want. It's everything you ever need, and it's here right in front of you." He wasn't talking about his circus show. No. This time, he realized that what he had always wanted was to connect with the people who love him, his family. He was talking about his less-than-famous daughter playing a small part in the school play. It wasn't about the amount of fame for him. It was about the amount of love for his daughter. It was about his "mosts."

My wife was sitting with me in the movie theater, and I thought of her. My kid was home with a babysitter, and I thought of him. Like P.T. Barnum, I struggle with the "I'm Not Enough" mentality. I've worried my whole life about being enough for the world, but the people who love me the most already think I am. I thought I needed to be perfect to be loved, but I just needed to love my imperfections. Love doesn't require perfection. It requires dedication to the person inside of you and in front of you.

What's your lie, and what's the fear behind your lie? Fill in the blank, "I'm not (blank) enough." What popped into your head: skinny enough, tall enough, funny enough, helpful enough, popular enough, successful enough, or rich enough? Maybe you're not enough of those things to be liked by everyone, but happiness isn't found in being liked by everyone. It's found in being loved by a few, including yourself.

I don't know you, but I do know whatever monsters you're fighting inside can be tamed by the love of one person who accepts you. Everyone needs at least one person who accepts them for who they are, but it won't matter how many people like you if you don't like yourself. Acceptance starts with you.

The actor and comedian Jim Carey once said, "I wish everyone could get rich and famous and have everything they ever dreamed of so that they will know that it's not the answer." Jim Carey is rich and famous, but he knows many miserable rich and famous people. Why? There is nothing wrong with wealth and fame, but it doesn't deliver the expected self-worth and joy. Focus on who you want to be on the inside.

SLAYING YOUR MONSTERS

Stop beating yourself up over dumb decisions made by your "Me-Monsters," but don't stay in the mud long after falling in. Imagine if one of your friends made a mistake and kept dwelling on it, or maybe someone hurt them, and they had a hard time getting over it. What would you tell them? Would you say, "Yup, stay in that mental hole for a few more years"? No. You would say, "That was tough, but I know you're tougher. You got this, and I got you. Get back up and own it."

Slaying your monsters takes brave action. Monsters aren't scared of the self-help books you read, but they fear what you do with them. First, stop doing things that are an oxymoron to the person you're trying to become. Stop feeding the beast snacks. Second, start doing things that feed the good wolf.

Here are some things you can do right away to feed your good wolf.

1. Dance silly in front of someone.

2. Mess up your hair and keep it that way for a while.

3. Kindly poke fun at yourself around others.

4. Congratulate someone who beats you at something.

5. Hug yourself, kiss your arm, and tell yourself, "I love you." (Probably privately)

MY FAITH

What helped me slay my monsters the most wasn't an app or online video. It wasn't even a self-help book. It was seeking God with my whole heart and receiving His love and forgiveness. I know our culture doesn't like talking about things like religion, but I would be doing the topic of this book a disservice if I didn't own the main thing that helped me overcome my monsters and gave me a better life.

In high school and college, I had popularity, girls, and success, but something was missing deep down. I wasn't sure if I believed in God, but I was ready to give Him a chance. One night while driving home after a college party filled with indulgences, I decided to rethink who I wanted to be. I said a prayer. I asked God to send me a girl I could be good to and who could be good for me. A few days later, Rachel, my future wife, messaged me online. She and I were each other's first boyfriend and girlfriend in fifth grade. We broke up in sixth grade, and I moved away. We rarely talked except for when I came back to visit friends. She just so happened to message me days after my prayer. That was more than a coincidence.

We reconnected and started dating even though she lived three hours away. She said she was a Christian and made some mistakes in college, but moving forward, she wanted to recommit to God. She wanted to wait to have sex until she got married. Being a playboy, I didn't think I could wait, but I also knew that the life I was living wasn't good for me.

Rachel and I started dating, and I researched Christianity. I found that there is evidence for God being real and Jesus being who He said He was, the savior of the world, the real Iron Man who took iron nails in His hands to forgive the sinful "marks" on my soul. After a few months of seeking with an open heart, I came to the humble realization that I was a sinner. I owned it. I wanted to be forgiven. Eventually, the wall fell within me, and I gave my life to Christ. I didn't hear "a voice" from God, but I felt His presence within. My heart grew bigger, and my ego grew smaller. I became better for myself and others because of an inner transformation. Rachel and I remained pure to each other until marriage, and we now have two beautiful, rambunctious boys.

I don't want my boys to live as I did as a teenager, taking risks that could land them in jail or with other long-term consequences. I want them to realize the Truth, receive God's love in their hearts, and live better lives. Rachel helped me see what truly matters the most: discovering God's love, accepting it, and letting it change me.

Having a better life sometimes requires you to first get tired of the lamer one. I chose to check my ego and change my ways. Rachel makes me better. God makes me better. I'm not trying to force my faith on you, but I'm not afraid to own it. I'm a work in progress who is saved by grace. I hope you will be inclusive and respect my story. I'm imperfect, but I own my imperfections and am loved by God despite them.

Face the monsters that cover your inner beauty. Know that you are wonderfully created and loved and are meant for good, not evil. Know that. Own that.

CHAPTER APPLICATION:

Own Your "Monsters"

1. Which "Me-Monsters" do you struggle with, and how can you take ownership of them?

2. Does your ego project an inflated view of yourself, a deflated view of yourself, or both at times? What is feeding your bad wolf?

3. What can you do this week to work on slaying your monsters?

CHAPTER 4

OWN THE GOOD, BAD, AND UGLY

∼

"If you're going to own it, own all of it."

-Brandon Lee White

OWN THE GOOD: Efforts and Accomplishments

Take time to realize all the good you've done. You've spent years working toward a high school or college diploma. Maybe you've already put in years at a current job, developing skills. You're growing your skills and contributing to a team and a higher cause. You're making money and providing for yourself and perhaps others. You're making memories with friends and living life. Celebrate that. Celebrate all the good in your life. Even if you're not collecting first-place trophies, you are growing through everything you put effort into. Be proud of who you're becoming and the effort you're making.

You don't have to be good at everything to celebrate. We all have shortcomings. I've met people who can't smile for the nine things they've done right because of the one thing they've done wrong. Come on! It's good to improve, but give yourself credit when credit is due, including effort. That progress is not wasted. You can build upon what you've already accomplished.

I'm more impressed with people's efforts than accomplishments. If someone super talented in something does well, so what? I applaud the person who grinds when it doesn't come naturally. So, celebrate the good in you and the good work from you.

OWN THE BAD: Tragedies and Mistakes

It's not a matter of if bad things will happen to you, but when. We don't want them, but if we're wise, we will become better because of them. Take ownership of bad things that happen and grow through them.

MY FRIEND CARL

About three years into my speaking career, I was invited to a special conference where students with disabilities were paired up with people doing what they wanted to do when they grew up. I was paired with a 19-year-old named Carl, who wanted to be a motivational speaker like me. Carl lived a normal life until his junior year in high school when he rode in the passenger seat with a friend to go to a party. It was a Thursday at 7:19 p.m. Carl's friend took a left turn at a yielding green light, but Carl's friend didn't yield to the oncoming SUV. Maybe it was a glare on the windshield, perhaps it was something she was looking at outside the window, or maybe it was something on her phone, but the SUV struck Carl's side at 60 mph. When the paramedics arrived, they thought Carl was dead until they detected faint breathing. They pried him out of the metal mess and airlifted him to the emergency room.

The doctor told Carl's family that he would probably have died if he had arrived at the hospital ten minutes later. Carl's face was completely smashed, with one of his eyes dislodged from its socket. He had numerous broken bones. He was in a coma for months, and when he awoke, he had brain damage, causing him to relearn how to walk and talk. Even though Carl was a Junior, he had memory loss and thought he was still a sophomore.

It was a long road to recovery for Carl, and he lost some of his so-called friends. Although Carl now has partial paralysis on the right side of his body, making him unable to drive, and although he has a minor speech impediment, he is a success story.

I was honored to help Carl build a website, and he delivered a professional speech at one of my events, where I shared the stage with him. Carl occasionally speaks at local schools about thinking first before making decisions. Carl even forgave his classmate who drove the car, and they are friends again.

Carl chooses his attitude. He makes fun of himself in a playful way. For example, he calls his walking with a limp his "swag walk." Carl has improved in all areas by putting in hard work with physical therapy.

After the accident, Carl could have quickly retreated into a hole and hid, but that's not what Carl did. He owned it. He owned a bad moment and repurposed it for good. He chose better attitudes of forgiving, optimistic, patient, grateful, humble, and brave. Carl likes a country song whose lyrics say, "If you're going through hell, keep on going." I'm proud of you, Carl! Love you, bro. Keep on going, and keep owning it.

The Taoist parable Sāi Wēng Lost His Horse tells of a poor Chinese farmer. The poor Chinese farmer lost a horse, and all the neighbors came around and said, "Well, that's too bad." The farmer said, "Maybe." Shortly after, the horse returned, bringing another horse with him, and all the neighbors came around and said, "Well, that's good fortune," to which the farmer replied, "Maybe." The next day, the farmer's son was trying to tame the new horse and fell, breaking his leg, and all the neighbors came around and said, "Well, that's too bad," and the farmer replied, "Maybe." Shortly after, the emperor declared war on a neighboring nation and ordered all able-bodied men to fight. Many died or became disabled, but the farmer's son was unable to fight and was spared due to his injury. All the neighbors came around and said, "Well, that's good fortune," to which the farmer replied, "Maybe."

We never know what will come from current events. We can only own them and make the best of them. Whether it's your fault or not, own it. Accept it and make the best of it. It's the only good option.

OWN THE UGLY: Social Media and Other Vices

We all have vices, things we overuse and misuse to feel good in the wrong way. They come from our bad wolves. These could be drugs, alcohol, food, video games, porn, social media, etc. Vices are harmful things we do to ourselves. Unlike mistakes, we know we're doing something unhealthy, yet we continue to do it. Vices rob us of healthy relationships with ourselves and others.

Let's talk about social media. Social media is great, but it's also not. It can get downright ugly. We often settle for watching other people's lives instead of living our own. If you're already shy, it can become something you hide behind because virtual friendships are easier than in-person ones.

Social media can confuse who you are with who you want to appear to be. We know it can propagate inauthenticity, superficiality, and insecurity. It's hard not to feel insecure and jealous when you see your friends posing on a beach during their vacation with their toned bodies and seemingly stress-free smiles. Meanwhile, maybe you're almost halfway through a cursed house project with screaming kids in the background and a new blood pressure record.

Social media breeds constant comparison and the desire for and means to fake who you are to impress others. In addition, social media is often used for bullying, identity theft, and other rotten things. This drains happiness. I distinctly remember numerous times binging on social media and not feeling good about myself afterward. Why do I keep going back, like, five minutes later?

I've never tried crack cocaine, but there have been times that I have looked at my screen time and understood it. I've been hooked. The addiction, the beast, salivates with each notification. What would your life even look like with less screen time? It would require more effort than scrolling but produce more wellness. It would make more time for hobbies, passions, friendships, exercise, reading, and rejuvenating relaxation.

Suppose you've been overly dependent on screens for entertainment and connection. In that case, real life will begin to appear unappealing, boring, and maybe even inferior. I remember my wife suggesting we cut back on technology as a family. The idea of taking a bike ride, reading a book, or having a board game night seemed boring. It's the addiction trying to hang on. When I detoxed my mind from technology, I reconnected to real life and experienced more energy, joy, and meaningful memories.

I'm not entirely anti-social media, but I take social media breaks and delete my apps for a week or more without deleting my account. Currently, I have my wife set time limits on social media apps, and she sets the password. Since I can't change the password, I can't sabotage myself and wreck my mental health through overusing screen time. Doing this makes me feel less distracted and less emotionally dependent on phone notifications to make me feel special. Sounds silly? Maybe for some, but I bet most of you know what I'm talking about and see the wisdom in my actions. I'm not letting the bad wolf have a chance. I'm being proactive by reducing distractions and addictive things. You can, too. Try it.

Our "ugly" choices go against who we want to be. Our list of vices and mistakes can be long, but the real tragedy is letting them demotivate you. It's so easy to get into a funk and shame yourself. No matter the vice, whether it's overeating, gossiping, inappropriate lusting, binge-screen watching, or substance abuse, the best thing you can do is own up to it, get help if you need it, and move in the right direction. When you feel the temptation coming on, say the phrase, "This is a moment to own it." Choose to do something else in that moment to shift your energy. Open a good book, watch an inspirational video, go outside, talk to a friend or counselor, or meditate/pray. Do what it takes to take ownership of your life.

If you're going to own it, own all of it: the good, the bad, and the ugly.

CHAPTER APPLICATION:
Own the Good, Bad, and Ugly

1. What are some of your "good," and how do you own it?

2. Find a way to celebrate something you've done recently.

3. What are some of your "bad," and how do you own it?

4. What are some of your "ugly," and how do you own it?

5. Have a friend or family member put the necessary filters on your phone.

CHAPTER 5

PROUD ACTIONS

~

"Hard work beats talent when talent doesn't work hard."

- Tim Notke (High School Basketball Coach)

Proud actions include doing the hard things that accomplish your "mosts" and make you feel proud. This improves the relationship with yourself by building confidence and dignity. "Proud actions" help you like yourself more. It's difficult to like yourself if you are not proud of yourself. You might think, "Wait, Brandon, what about just loving ourselves?" Yes! Love yourself even if you're a hot mess but love yourself enough not to stay there. You owe it to yourself and the people around you to continually mature and grow because that yields the greatest return not only in production but also in enjoyment and fulfillment. Make something of yourself. Everyone should desire being able to say before going to bed at night, "I'm proud of who I'm becoming." The key word is "becoming." Proud actions help you become that.

THE SHY KID WITH A SPEECH IMPEDIMENT

A kindergartener sat alone during recess. None of the other kids talked to or played with him. Although the boy was shy, he had tried to speak to the other kids, but many ignored him. He sat there alone and wondered why no one liked him.

One day, when the parents arrived at the preschool to pick him up, the teacher told them, "Your son has a speech impediment, and the other students can't understand him. It would be best if you put him in speech therapy." His mother was worried. What would this do to her son's self-esteem? How would he transition back to school?

In a small room, the speech therapist said, "Repeat after me. The red rabbit ran up the road." The boy squirmed in his seat before meekly repeating, "Wa wed wabbit wan up the woad." He was frustrated and mad for not being able to talk clearly. So, he spoke gibberish on purpose—and then stopped talking altogether. The teacher said, "Try again." He didn't say a word. His parents asked, "How was school?" He looked at the ground in silence and retreated to his room.

He went to bed, woke up, and nothing changed. He knew what he had to do: own it. He returned to speech class and said, "Wabbit, wabbit, wabbit," with a new-found determination. One day at the end of the school year, the boy grit his teeth, took a breath, and finally, "The red rabbit ran up the road."

He went back to school with the students who made fun of him, but he decided not to be like them. He decided to use his voice for good. That shy kid with a speech impediment was me.

I was a kid who couldn't speak, and now I am a nation-wide professional speaker. How does that happen? It happened because I owned my "marks" and my "mosts," and I chose "proud actions." There was the moment when I refused to speak, but then there was the "proud action" where I decided to own it and get to work. There was the moment when I wanted to settle for a career that was not right for me, but then there was the "proud action" where I owned my dream to be a motivational speaker. There was the moment when I doubted if I should write this book and my ability to do so, but then there was the "proud action" of committing the time and grinding out sentence after sentence.

PROGRESS

How do you get motivated to do what you need to do? Progress. A lack of progress demotivates. Studies show that when people feel they're progressing at something, it's easier for them to keep going. The problem is that people get discouraged when they aren't progressing, so they give up. Like water finding the path of least resistance, it's easy to slide down the hill. Conversely, climbing a mountain-- heck, walking up a flight of stairs takes small intentional steps. If you know you're getting closer to the desired result, it's easier to persevere. Furthermore, I go to bed proud if I know I'm progressing, but I'm uneasy when I feel stuck and going in circles.

I'm getting better at speaking Spanish, and it's because of the app Duolingo. I'm so impressed with it. It seems to take all the dopamine-hitting strategies that things like slot machines and video games use and apply them to something useful; learning a new language. I can set my daily goals. Currently, I have it at the 5-minute-a-day minimum. It shows my daily streak on my phone's home screen, and it has dopamine-pleasing bells and whistles with each completed lesson. It starts easy and gradually increases in difficulty. This maintainable pace of progress maintains my confidence and motivation to continue. I actually look forward to the next day's lesson. Consider various apps and tools for all your goals. Use the available technology to give you an advantage.

THE COMFORT TRAP

What do people really want in life? To make a difference? To get a great education? To make money? To make deep friendships? Sure. But many are willing to trade it all for one thing: comfort. Great things are often traded for easy things. The irony is that when we avoid discomfort, we create discomfort. I could avoid my responsibilities and watch TV and eat chips, but I would get unhealthy, feel guilty, and miss out on life. Taking breaks is fine, but don't fall for the comfort trap.

Refuse to get lured into the addiction of comfort that shallows out happiness. Remember, settling too much in life makes for an unsettled life. Psychologist Jordan Peterson said, "You can choose frivolous fun for your life, but you won't have meaning. You can have meaning, but it comes with responsibility."

The good news is that you don't have to do it alone. In fact, you shouldn't. I received help from my speech teacher. The same is true with my speaking career. What is something you're struggling with, and who might be able to help you? Go talk to them.

GRIT

Do you push yourself even when you want to give up? You can't be proud of yourself and truly like yourself without pushing yourself, which is how you develop grit. "Proud actions" require grit. Grit is sticking with something hard until it gets easier. You are capable of so much. Too many people give up too soon. When I first got married, my wife expected me to know how to fix things. She was sadly mistaken. I could have settled with the lame, familiar story of, "I'm just not good at fixing things." Instead, I grabbed my phone and learned.

The first time I replaced a chandelier in my house, I thought I just performed brain surgery. It was hard. When I replaced the second one, it was easier. I could have given in

"The irony is that when we avoid discomfort, we create discomfort."

to the "now" feeling of frustration when trying to figure out the different colored wires, but I didn't. I'm proud to look back on the moments when I fixed or built something. Life is hard, but it's harder when you don't know squat and can't do squat. Learn to do things.

Doing hard things convinces your brain that you can do hard things. Some people are born ready to audition for American Idol. Good for them, but you benefit little from that which comes easy. It's in the grind that you find the growth.

Two-A-Days in football and grueling runs in cross-country made me a stronger person. Math never came easy to me, either. One semester in college, I pushed myself harder than ever, and when I received that test paper declaring an "A," it was a feeling like none other. Inside, I felt that I could do hard things. Every time you give up, as soon as it gets difficult, you're building a habit of giving up. Stay in the discomfort to get stronger.

Try a cold shower. I know. I hate cold water, too. I'm the baby of babies with cold water, but this will train your brain to stay in discomfort. Start at medium temperature. You don't have to go all out freezing. Your brain will start screeching at the cooler water. Remind yourself that you are not in danger and that it is temporary discomfort. Think of the cold water as simply a sensation, which it is. Nothing is cutting or burning your skin. It's just your brain overreacting. Desensitize your brain to the discomfort. Say, "It's just a sensation." Cold showers have good benefits, such as decreased depression, better circulation, faster metabolism, etc. Try it.

The name of my nonprofit, which hosts various leadership conferences, is "Love the Tough." I love the tough, not for what it is, but for what it makes me: tougher. We must teach people in America to "Love the tough" instead of "Find the shortcut." People want public praise without private perseverance. For all the good AI will do, it might do too much because just like the cocoon strengthens the butterfly by making it work to escape, embracing life's challenges makes us better suited for it.

The philosopher G. Michael Hopf said, "Hard times

create strong men. Strong men create good times. Good times create weak men. And weak men create hard times." Our country wants everything quick and easy. Easy is what we want, but tough is what we need. We want good grades, but we need to study. We want victories, but we need practice. We want good friendships, but we need to have tough conversations during conflict. We want money, but we need to work. Why? External challenge produces internal strength. Internal strength produces external results.

Mediocrity is where the majority live. I've done my fair share of shoddy things. I've created, delivered, and performed things on par with kindergarten artwork. While in pre-school, my youngest kid was told to color a picture, and he simply scribbled green over the whole image. Was it colored? Yes. Was it lazy and pathetic? Yes. I still love you, son.

"Proud actions" include putting in a solid effort. You know that feeling of turning in half-baked homework. It's like when you share your drink with someone, but it's the last sip. We know that's mostly backwash! Maybe that's a myth. I don't know. My point is that the quality of what you do matters. It shapes how you feel about yourself, how the world treats you, and the impact you leave. The temptation is to slack like everyone else, but you don't want a life like everyone else.

Get really good at your job. You will be paid more, enjoy it more, and be respected more. Get good at things and get really good at a few things. Be able to produce pure excellence in something that matters to you. I've applied myself more to writing this book than any other book I wrote. Every time I felt like scribbling green and calling it good, I reopened the laptop and kept grinding. I'm creating something excellent because that's what the reader deserves.

Remember that almost everything great started as something not-so-great. Flip phones used to be the best phone technology mankind could create, but we stayed with it and progressed to much better. It's the 20th draft of a book, the 5,000th free throw, and the friendship that you work through that ends up being great. What have you done that you can call great? Don't give an excuse. You are capable of greatness. Own it.

FOCUS ON YOUR STRENGTHS

What are your strengths? Are they being organized, reading body language, communicating with tact, staying positive, maintaining ambition, demonstrating empathy, researching and processing data, committing to people or a cause, finding the fun and bringing the energy, being bold and assertive, or maintaining peace and defusing conflict? The upcoming chapter on personality types may help you discover those strengths.

> "It's difficult to like yourself if you're not proud of yourself."

You don't have to be excellent at everything. Improve your weaknesses, but focus on your strengths. For example, if you're not a naturally funny person, don't stress about it. Try to loosen up and find some humor, but know it's not your core strength. You won't be the funniest person, nor do you have to be. If you're not a great communicator, or if you're painfully introverted, focus on how you can support and influence in a way you're comfortable with. With all of this said you can improve upon these perceived weaknesses. Don't simply settle. Improve your weaknesses but focus on your strengths.

Get good at many things, really good at a few things, and make better moments that you're proud of. Have something to show for your life. Suck it up, buttercup. You can do hard things. You're stronger than you realize. You're a bad mama jama, whatever that means.

CHAPTER APPLICATION:

"Proud Actions"

1. What are some things you've done that you're proud of?

2. If you work a job, how can you get better at it?

3. What's something you want to get great at doing?

4. What are your strengths, and how can you continue to develop them?

CHAPTER 6

BETTER ATTITUDES

~

"Choosing your attitude isn't about forcing fake feelings; it's about bravely dealing with the real ones."

- Brandon Lee White

Achieving "proud actions" requires emotional intelligence to identify your bad attitudes and choose better ones. Bad attitudes are one of the biggest causes of bad relationships. We're all guilty. We get angry, lazy, jealous, and so on. Humans and animals are a lot alike. Both can learn, build, and even feel, but humans can choose the kind of humans they want to be. We can wake up and say, "Today, I will be better." That's the mentality of owning it.

Choosing your attitude is not about forcing fake feelings; it's about bravely dealing with the real ones. Own them. It's not about faking smiles or memorizing cheesy inspirational quotes. It's about getting real with the side of you that is working against you: your bad wolf and "Me-Monsters." This chapter helps you identify negative attitudes and choose better ones.

I define a bad attitude as habitual negative thinking that turns into negative behavior. For example, jealousy starts with the idea that you would be happier if you had what someone else has. This belief creates envy. If you don't respond wisely to these feelings, you can develop a jealous attitude that becomes a habit. This becomes part of who you are rather than a temporary feeling.

Someone may be born with a tendency toward a certain bad attitude. If you don't manage the natural tendency, it will form a habit. Imagine a dirt road with two tire ruts from the trucks going back and forth over time. These ruts sink deeper, making it harder to avoid them. We must be aware of the ruts we have formed over time because they can cause unnecessary conflict within ourselves and with others. For example, whenever you blow up in anger, you create a deeper habit of anger. Whenever you procrastinate on your responsibilities, you create a deeper habit of laziness.

Again, choosing your attitude is not about forcing fake feelings; it's about bravely dealing with the real ones. Get good at detecting when the bad attitude starts rearing its ugly Madusa-like head. This is called awareness. When you know you are feeling a bad attitude, pause the moment and deal with it. The goal is not to never get angry but to be able to process the feeling and prevent it from becoming a habit. The same is true about slowing down a positive moment. When you are aware of a special moment, you can slow it down and savor it. Anytime a consequential event or opportunity is about to happen, say, "This is a moment to own it." Slow it down and choose the right response.

Your attitude is the thermostat, and your feeling is the thermometer. The thermometer reads what it is, but the thermostat can change what it is. You may feel one way, but you can take ownership and choose your attitude. Much of what people think of you is based on the attitude you display toward them. It reflects what is inside you, or at least how you manage it. By choosing a positive attitude, you're choosing a positive spokesperson to represent your brand; that is, you.

Here are common bad attitudes and their opposing better ones. Which of the following bad attitudes do you struggle with? I struggle with being impatient. Which "better attitudes" come naturally to you? For me, I'm stronger in the forgiving, optimistic, and disciplined attitudes.

Bad Attitudes:
1. Angry
2. Pessimistic
3. Impatient
4. Jealous
5. Arrogant
6. Lazy
7. Shy

Better Attitudes:
1. Forgiving
2. Optimistic
3. Patient
4. Grateful
5. Humble
6. Disciplined
7. Outgoing

Bad Attitude 1:

Angry

Out-of-control anger spreads like fire, burning bridges, scorching the heart, and leaving a pile of ashy loneliness and regret. Anger threatens your relationships, goals, future career, and happiness.

Yes, I can have an anger problem. I can turn into the Hulk and smash my keyboard when the power goes out because I forgot to turn auto-save back on and lost 58 minutes of work on my Word document. I become like Scrat, the squirrel in the Ice Age movies who almost gets the acorn but is left with a twitching eye and an imminent emotional outburst.

Anger comes from feeling wronged, disrespected, or disappointed. It can include annoyance, irritability, sarcasm, sassiness, vengefulness, and rage like the "Exploder Me-Monster." It can be passive or active. You have an expectation of how you want something to go or how you want someone to act, and when expectations don't match reality, you can get angry or at least annoyed. The negative feelings can build over the years, like magma under a volcano.

If you choose an attitude of anger, people will know you for what you're against. Our relationships are always better when we are more known for what we are for rather than what we are against. For example, you could rant about how you hate this or that all day. OK, we get it, but what are you actually for? You are way better to be around when you promote the positive things you want rather than the negative things that upset you.

Getting easily offended and triggered with anger can be a sign of unresolved conflict and trauma from your past. This book is not meant to replace the role of a professional psychiatrist or counselor. Seek a professional if necessary. Talking about feelings is like physical therapy for the soul.

We are all on the spectrum of "anti-people." Even if you're a nice person, you have a limit. You are human; human nature is self-preservation first and love thy neighbor second. Have you ever been let down by a friend or, worse, sabotaged? Do you have a family member who consistently puts their needs above yours? Have you taken time to help someone or generously given them something and not even received a "Thank you" in return? Is there someone bullying you? If people want to, they can be mean to you, and you can be mean to them. It's free will. The problem is that you may yell, pout, complain, become sassy, or give the silent treatment, but it doesn't make you happier in the end.

Pixar's movie Elemental has a great quote where Wade, the water guy, says, "When I lose my temper, I think it's just me trying to tell myself something I'm not ready to hear." Isn't that true? Like a toddler, our inner self throws a tantrum when our expectations don't align with the truth of reality. When I get upset, I don't want to hear the truth. I want to vent my feelings. The first step to fixing a problem is admitting you have one. Listen to the truth.

I believe the truth in resolving anger is that forgiveness is more effective than bitterness. First, let me say that forgiveness doesn't excuse what happened. They still might face natural or legal consequences, but you are relinquishing yourself from the job of the judge and executioner. You may think punishing someone for hurting you will feel better than forgiving them. It doesn't. Creating pain in others doesn't heal yours. Forgiveness is wanting the best for someone, which can include them learning their lesson. Still, you may not be able to trust that person until they earn your trust back. Hopefully, you can restore the relationship. Regardless, free yourself from the raging fire of anger that chars the soul.

BROKEN GLASS

It was the summer of 2010, and I was running some downtown errands. It was the middle of the day when I went inside a building, but by the time I came out, cop cars were around my SUV. My back window was busted out. The cop said a guy broke into your back window to steal something, but we got him before he got away. I saw a broken window with glass everywhere, but then I saw a broken-looking man in the back of the cop car in handcuffs. The officer told me that he just got out of jail and was trying to make a quick buck by stealing. What he did was wrong, and I knew that window would cost a lot to repair, $400 to be exact, but at that *moment, I didn't feel angry. I only felt sorrow for the man in the back of the cop car. What has he been through? What will happen to him? Does he have a family? How much longer will he be in jail?*

A feeling came over me, and then an idea. I told the officer to wait. I went inside my vehicle and grabbed a spare Bible. "Here," I told the officer, "Give this to the man and tell him I forgive him." The officer looked at me surprised and then smiled. I watched as the man took the Bible and briefly looked at me through the back of the cop car window.

Did he think that he didn't deserve my forgiveness? Was he angry at the cops? Was he angry at himself? Was he scared? I'm unsure what he felt, but I know what I felt. Free. I felt free from anger.

That's what forgiveness does. It frees. Instead of swatting at a bumblebee, it opens the window to let it out. So, when you see the broken glass left behind by the people who hurt you, make sure you also see the broken people. We are all broken in one way or another and need forgiveness. It touches people's hearts, and it starves the bad wolf. It's about loving people, not always in a best-friend way but in a wanting-the-best-for-them way. As for me, not everyone deserves my forgiveness, but I'm better when I give it. It makes for a better moment, a better story, and a better life.

Do you have anger toward a relative or friend? Have they done something hurtful? Forgiveness starts with perspective. I love what Jesus said while he was unjustly tortured on a cross with nails driven through his hands and feet, "Father, forgive them because they don't know what they do." It moves me to know that Jesus was willing to see the ignorance of others behind their offenses. He knew that they just didn't "get it."

> "That's what forgiveness does. It frees. Instead of swatting at a bumblebee, it opens the window to let it out."

You have some options. If they're unwilling to apologize or talk about it, keep them at arm's length while being kind. If they sincerely apologize, grant them forgiveness and a chance to rebuild your trust. Realize that people will offend you, and you will eventually offend others. We're messy, sinful people, but we can learn and grow with the help of some grace.

Better Attitude: Forgiving

__Bad Attitude 2:__

Pessimistic

We all have a negativity bias. We tend to focus on the negative more than the positive. Don't believe me? Consider the reason why news stations seem to report constant bad news. People tune in to bad news more than good news. Unfortunately, this same negativity bias is why we focus on what we don't like in the mirror and why we doubt our potential. To make it worse, negativity can spread. You can make others negative. What's the solution? Work out your pessimism by making yourself take positive risks that prove the negativity bias wrong.

WHEEL OF FORTUNE

My wife and I sat on our couch watching Wheel of Fortune. A thought crossed my mind. We could win. I saw people winning and thought, "Why not us?" I turned to my wife and said, "Let's audition." She rolled her eyes and said, "Yeah, right." Undeterred, I grabbed my phone and went to the Wheel of Fortune website to submit a video audition. "Hi! My name is Brandon, and my wife and I think we can win Wheel of Fortune. Choose us!" I put my phone down and turned to see my wife shaking her head in doubt.

One week later...

"Congratulations!" the email said, "You've been selected to attend a live audition in Kansas City!" I was beaming with glory as I showed my wife. Again, she rolled her eyes and said, "They send those emails to everyone."

A couple of weeks later...

We went to the live audition and tried our best. I could see the hope slowly growing within my wife, but she was afraid to get her hopes too high.

A few weeks later, I was about to confess that my wife was right when we received "the email." "Congratulations, you've been chosen to be on Wheel of Fortune!" I jumped up and down like a 6-year-old at a birthday party, but my wife's face resembled that of the anxious parent in the back corner of the party, waiting for something to break or spill. She was afraid of embarrassing herself on national television. I understand that. Just look up videos of "Wheel of Fortune Fails."

Fear focuses on what might happen, but courage focuses on what needs to happen. Sure, we *might lose, but we need go after once-in-a-life-time opportunities. We researched how to win Wheel of Fortune and found out the acronym to remember is EAT IRONS. Starting with "E" is the most common letter and ending with "S." But, if the theme of the puzzle is "Things," guess an "S" because "Things" will always be plural. The theme, "What are you doing?" will always have an I-N-G.*

We flew out to Los Angeles with Rachel's mother. Pat Sajak was witty and kind, and Vanna White was lovely and approachable. They record only one day a week and do all six shows in one day. We were slotted for the fifth show, which gave us time to get nervous. We walked onto the stage in awe and excitement. Everything looked smaller in person. There were about 100 people seated on an upper balcony, including my mother-in-law.

The game included crazy ups and downs and a little luck. We ended up winning the "prize puzzle" to Disney World and the final Bonus Round for a grand total of $60,500! Before taxes! Haha, we ended up with about $28,000 cash and a trip to see Mickey.

That night, my wife, mother-in-law, and I ate

*at a fancy hotel restaurant and ordered steak
and wine. Afterward, we soaked in the jacuzzi
and our glory. It was one of the most exciting
days of my life, and the crazy part is it almost
didn't happen. When my wife said, "Yeah,
right," while sitting on the couch, someone else
said it, too: me. My negativity bias threatened
to erase everything: the memories, the money,
and The Magic Kingdom.*

How much has your negativity bias taken from you? What opportunities have you missed out on? Do you live in a mind dominated by nonstop "What ifs?" Do you almost always choose the less risky option? Would you prefer not to embarrass yourself over possibly doing something fun and accomplishing something meaningful? What would you try if you knew you couldn't fail or get embarrassed? With all this said, there is such a thing as "toxic positivity," which is being overly optimistic. It says, "Oh, don't worry about it. You're fine. We don't need to worry or talk about it or plan." This naïve attitude can lead you to dangerous and dumb decisions. Be optimistic, but don't ignore the truth.

What does an optimistic attitude look like in the workplace? It looks like acknowledging problems but focusing on solutions. It looks like contributing to brainstorming and collaboration rather than blaming and isolation. It looks like getting excited about possibilities and knowing you play a part in making them a reality. It looks like giving people second chances, when appropriate, and seeing the best in them. It looks like refusing to excessively complain and cut down people and ideas. It looks like positive influence, not negative influence.

Better Attitude: Optimistic

Bad Attitude 3:

Impatient

When I wrote my novel *Freshman Wisdom*, I was impatient. I ordered a large pallet of my books and was proud until I read a copy. The first typo I noticed was in the first chapter. "Hmm," I thought, "I guess one got overlooked." Then, there were two typos in chapter two, and so on, throughout the book. I was embarrassed to realize that I had spent all that time and money to write a great book, but now the book's overall quality was tainted with typos. I relaunched a revised edition, but it reminded me of a valuable lesson. Haste makes waste.

Impatience can come from the unwillingness to delay gratification or the desire for immediate certainty. For me, I value efficiency. So, I get impatient when I feel something is inefficient. I don't want to waste my time or energy. For example, yesterday a car slowed down to turn and took longer than I approved. I said, "Come on! Turn!" out loud to myself. Silly right? Getting frustrated and venting to myself didn't help the situation. You may say, "Yeah, but it feels good to complain!" The problem is that it becomes a habit. You train yourself to be easily discontent and annoyed. The opposite is true that we can train ourselves to be more content and accepting of the moment and the people in it.

Try this. Leave five minutes early and deliberately walk or drive slower. Let people pass in front of you. Microwave something for 1-2 minutes and patiently look at the microwave the entire time. Your bad wolf will be yapping the whole time. Take some deep breaths when you start feeling impatient. Patience is accepting what is instead of needing to over-control what you want to be. Impatience is an unappreciation of the current moment. Don't undervalue the mundane moments because when you're old and close to dying, you realize how precious each moment is. Besides, everyone wants to be happy, right? The happiest people are the ones who learn to be patient and content in a variety of situations and moments.

Regarding relationships, author Stephen Covey said, "With people, fast is slow, and slow is fast." If you rush through conflict, trying to force a good relationship, you're having the opposite effect. Instead, be patient and talk through things. Give people second chances when appropriate. Give them options and space to think and make their own decisions. Give them attention and time when listening. Give the relationship time to grow.

Relationships stay shallow with impatient attitudes. Only through patience do relationships have the necessary environment for the roots to grow deeply and produce fruit. The bad attitude of anger often starts with impatience. I'm not saying to be lazy. You can still be diligent without rushing. You can be assertive with people without disregarding them. Be quick to listen, slow to speak, and slow to become angered, and you will unlock massive influence on others.

Better Attitude: Patient

Bad Attitude 4:

Jealous

Jealousy is about wanting what someone else has. Remember the saying, "Be content enough to accept the things you can't change, courageous enough to change the things you need to change, and wise enough to know the difference." Often, things we are jealous of are things we don't need. They are things that we want, usually, because we care too much about what others think. Try this: Think of five things you're grateful for and would be sad if they were taken away. For me, it's my family, house, job, ability to walk/talk/smell/taste/hear/ see, and overall good health. I also like to occasionally visit graveyards. It seriously puts things into perspective. You're still alive. Your time is not up, yet. You have much to be grateful for.

Another source of jealousy is comparison. I've heard it said that comparison is the thief of joy. With social media, it's no secret that we compare more so than previous generations. Set screen time limits on your social media or even unplug by deleting your apps for a week or month. If that thought freaks you out, that's a sign you're addicted. Tech addiction is a real thing. Don't treat it like it's not. Beyond jealousy, it creates all sorts of unhealthy imbalances in relationships. Own it. Don't let it own you. Once you limit unnecessary sources of comparison, you will experience more content and gratefulness.

Better Attitude: Grateful

Bad Attitude 5:

Arrogant

Arrogance is the exaggerated sense of one's importance or abilities. It comes from the unhealthy ego and can be found in the "Bragger Me-Monster." Unlike healthy pride, arrogance has little regard for others, expecting to be worshiped and served without reciprocating equal treatment. People can be arrogant in many ways. It could be how smart, athletic, rich, or good-looking they think they are compared to others.

There have been times when my wife and I have fought due to our arrogance. One time, we read a marriage book that gave advice on what to do in arguments. It said to hold hands, look at each other, and consider the other person's point of view. It felt so awkward, but we did it. After a few seconds, we couldn't help but laugh at how dumb we were acting. Humility melted our arrogance.

Humility is the only cure for arrogance, but it isn't easy to teach. Humility is not thinking less of yourself. It's simply thinking of yourself less. It means realizing that the world doesn't revolve around you and that people matter as much as you do. It means sharing, apologizing, and serving.

Humility grows through action. My wife watched Slumdog Millionaire, which is loosely based on the true story of a poor Indian man who, against the odds, won $1,000,000 on a game show. The movie made my wife realize the extreme poverty in other countries. She was humbled and felt compassion for people living in poverty. She decided to do something by sponsoring a child through World Vision. She developed a more humble, grateful, and generous attitude. We didn't know we would soon experience that third-world poverty in person.

HONDURAS

My wife and I went on a mission trip to Honduras to help bring students new school supplies. The trip took me out of my comfort zone. Honduras is partially known for its wild drivers, curvy roads, and vehicular deaths. Over two hours later, we made it to our destination alive with only a car-sick wife. Our hosts were very welcoming, and it was fun trying the local cuisine until I spent one of the nights puking my guts out from water pesticide exposure.

I was annoyed, fearful, ungrateful, a little angry, and a few other things. When I met the young students, they didn't speak much English. My Spanish is not as good as I pretend, but I realized something. Kids are kids. No matter the culture or language, kids are kids. I grabbed a soccer ball and said, "Futball?" They all cheered as we played soccer without words. Next, I taught them "Duck, Duck, Goose," but they didn't un-

derstand my English. So, I said, "Uno, Uno, Uno, Uno, Dose!" Haha. Weird, I know, but they loved it.

Keep in mind we played on dirt floors in an impoverished village made of mud huts with no running water, toilet systems, air conditioning, or convenience stores. They had a community water well, simple foods, and each other. Ironically, the kids were happy. The smiles and laughter didn't convey negative, whiny attitudes. Instead, they conveyed contentment and joy.

The positivity rubbed off on all of us, including my wife, who gifted a new pair of sandals to an elderly man named Pedro, who desperately needed them. She also bought a colorful hammock made by a blind man who plays guitar. I'm not sure how he does either of those, but it's beautiful.

When we arrived back in The United States, I felt like kissing the ground because I was grateful for our standard of living, but I also longed for something left behind. They didn't have much, but they had time with each other. They indeed had an inclusive village rather than closed-off subdivisions. They had positive attitudes even through their troubled circumstances.

The experience changed me. It made me appreciate what I have while realizing that there is more to life than money. It made me more grateful and generous. It humbled me.

Better Attitude: Humble

Brandon Lee White | 83

Bad Attitude 6:

Lazy

Laziness is a smooth talker and a robber of joy. I've been enticed by its crafty lies, such as "Maybe next week. It's too hard." Laziness creates discomfort by avoiding discomfort. You can avoid the discomfort of responsibilities, but you will create discomfort from their respective consequences.

Sleep, hydration, nutrition, tech time, and exercise all contribute to our energy levels and the laziness that may follow. As someone with low energy often, I've found that movement can create energy. This may be a walk or doing something productive. If I feel in a slump, I'll switch up what I'm doing and take a short break to get a healthy drink or snack. I might even splash some cold water on my neck and face, which can help you snap out of a lazy spell. I've also found that my attire effects my mood. Working at home in sweatpants lowers my motivation, whereas getting dressed up and looking good gives me confidence and motivation to work.

Where do you find the motivation when you feel lazy? You may be lacking purpose. Do you understand the meaning and impact of your work? Are you producing a product or providing a resource that helps improve lives? Are you making phone calls or connecting solutions to people's problems? If you can't articulate the purpose of your work, it won't energize you.

Are you working with people who energize and encourage you? This one is tougher to change, but it starts with being the change you want to see and "putting the right people on the bus," as Jim Collins says in *Good to Great*. A negative unappreciative culture drains motivation and breeds laziness. It's essential that you and leadership communicate purpose, appreciation, and support. Furthermore, building relationships and having connective relationships energize people. How can you create more of this within your capacity? We will discuss this further in Part Two.

A lazy attitude becomes overwhelmed by tasks. There are unavoidable tasks you must do as daily life, but prioritize what you can delay and what you should not. For example, I weed eat my yard every other mow. I prefer to buy groceries in bulk for fewer trips to the store. I make many purchases online so that I don't have to go to the store. I place things to go upstairs at the bottom step throughout the day, and only take them up when I go up.

I delegate chores to my kids to empower them and save my energy. My older son takes the trash out, loads the dishwasher, and sorts the laundry. My younger son wipes the tables and islands, vacuums rugs with a handheld vacuum, and picks up clutter such as toys and shoes. I have a close relationship with my sons and show them love. Therefore, teaching them to work is not a punishment; it's a gift of developing discipline. Their help lightens my load, reserves my energy, and makes my other responsibilities less daunting.

Life is too short and too awesome to waste. You have so

many things to do in your life that will help others and bring you joy. Don't let yourself keep you from living that. Be the best you. Get determined, be ambitious, and stay focused. You're worth it.

Better Attitude: Disciplined

Bad Attitude 7:

Shy

Shyness says, "I'm not enough to be seen and heard." It blocks the connection you're meant to experience with others. Shyness is the tendency to feel awkward or afraid around others because of insecurity and low self-esteem. Shyness could appear as the "Distancer Me-Monster."

Perhaps you think you're just being nice by not wanting to take any attention away from others. Maybe you want others to be happy, and, in your mind, you may say, "It doesn't matter if people hear me. It doesn't matter if I don't get my way. I just want others to be happy. I'll be quiet and stay out of the way." This might seem selfless, but it can quickly become self-limiting and self-destructive. It robs the world of what you have to offer.

Shyness is not the same as introversion. Introversion can be a strength, but shyness is a weakness. Shyness is being nervous or timid around people. Introverts might enjoy being with people, but it is usually at smaller doses and with fewer people. Being around people drains their energy, and they need to be alone to recharge. There is nothing wrong with being an introvert. I am more of an introvert than an extrovert. Introverts are good at observing others, understanding emotions, and regulating behavior.

Shyness is based on fear, which is meant to protect you and keep you from doing risky things, but the problem is that to have a better life, you must take risks and make good relationships. The fear you think is protecting you can end up harming you because it keeps you from connecting, loving, and growing. A life that is too safe, meaning without risks, is dangerous. It's not a danger to survival but to living. Don't let one bad event you had with people convince you that you're safer alone.

Much of shyness is in the mind. Consider this lie, "Everyone is looking at me and won't like who I am." First, everyone is not looking at you unless you do something really embarrassing, like splitting your pants on stage during a speech. True story. It happened to me at a presentation I gave to an elementary school. I just made sure I didn't turn around for the rest of the speech, and then the principal found some black duct tape that matched my black jeans and patched them up before the next show. Dang you, skinny jeans.

Pick a friend who is more outgoing than you and do something with them that stretches your comfort level. For example, sing a karaoke song or make an online video together. Lean on their courage to build yours, but you must practice bravery to become braver. Another exercise is talking to the mirror. Practice saying to the mirror, privately, what you are too shy to say to someone's face publically. This could relate to dating, promotions, opinions, ideas, etc.

Don't let yourself keep you from being yourself. Be brave. Let your light shine. The world needs it.

Better Attitude: Brave

CHAPTER APPLICATION:

Better Attitudes

1. **Forgiving**
   - Consider seeing a counselor to discuss your anger.
   - Take five minutes to consider forgiving someone who has wronged you.

2. **Optimistic**
   - Pick one short-term goal that can be achieved in less than a year and go after it.

3. **Patient**
   - Leave five minutes early to where you are going and deliberately walk or drive slower.

4. **Grateful**
   - List things you appreciate that you have.

5. **Humble**
   - Practice humility by seeking to understand in the middle of a conflict.

6. **Disciplined**
   - Identify the purpose of your work, prioritize your tasks, delegate when possible.

7. **Brave**
   - Don't cover up who you are with shyness. Be brave and share something authentic with the world.

CHAPTER 7

BETTER MENTAL HEALTH

~

"Asking for help isn't giving up. It's refusing to give up."

-Charley Mackesy (Author)

Mental health affects attitudes, which affect relationships. I've struggled with mental health since my early twenties. Many negative attitudes can be made worse by poor mental health. Sometimes, poor mental health requires professional help because you can't just "snap out of it." I empathize with anyone struggling with mental illness, but I know it's not hopeless.

MY DEPRESSION

I was 24 years old, and life was great. I was

beginning my career as a motivational speaker. I just got engaged to my fiancé, now my wife. Soon after the proposal, I started experiencing symptoms of depression. I woke up sad, unmotivated, irritable, and tired. I wasn't suicidal, but I couldn't imagine living the rest of my life like that. I remember waking up and not wanting to get out of bed. I thought I would feel more energetic if I took a nap. It never worked. The fatigue never went away. I drank energy drinks and coffee, but nothing seemed to help. Rachel still married me even though I was depressed, not knowing the future.

When our first child was born, I was so depressed that I often didn't want to play with him. I remember not wanting to talk to my wife. I remember not wanting to do anything. I was there, but not "there." My wife didn't understand. She thought I just needed to "snap out of it." I would retreat to a couch or my bed. Sometimes, we would yell at each other because we felt frustrated and misunderstood. Our marriage might have ended if it wasn't for our commitment to each other and our faith in God.

A couple of years into the depression, I saw a doctor and started taking an anti-depressant. After three months of no progress, I decided to quit because I was concerned about the side effects and withdrawals that anti-depression medication can cause—with that said, I'm not a doctor, and I'm not telling you what to do. I tried other possible solutions, such as light therapy and natural supplements. Nothing seemed to fully work for me. I was able to manage and even cover it up around friends. At my school speeches, I felt like a clown who was putting on an act. I would smile, put on a show, and then zone out in my hotel, watching TV for hours.

After five years of depression, I found a supplement that helped called SAM-E. I was managing better, but not entirely well. After six years of depression, I tried an elimination diet in which I eliminated all possible foods that could create sensitivities. I discovered that I was sensitive to gluten, and after eliminating it, I felt much better. I woke up, and for the first time in a long time, I felt like genuinely smiling and jumping with energy. My wife couldn't believe it. She didn't know if I was acting. It had been so long since she remembered the man that she got engaged to versus the depressed man she married. We hugged each other and cried. I cried for joy for having myself back, and I cried in sorrow, knowing how much time I lost.

Since then, I've been able to eat more gluten without side effects. I still struggle, at times, with energy and my mental health when I take certain medications, overeat sugar, drink too much alcohol, etc. I've learned how to manage my mental health. I'm not a doctor, and I'm not suggesting anything to you other than to seek help and not give up.

One of the best things for me was having someone there for me, even if she couldn't fix it. My wife learned to have more compassion, and she asked me one time, "What is it like having depression?" At that moment, she wasn't trying to fix me. She was trying to understand me. Her empathy didn't remove my depression, but it made it easier to live with it, knowing someone was willing to step into it with me. She was willing to sit with me in my pain and seek to understand. That's love.

If you are struggling with mental illness of any kind, find someone who will listen when you're ready to talk. If you know someone going through mental illness, be that someone for them. Always seek professional help along the way.

Structure your life in a way that supports your mental health. Balance work and play. Have friends who support you. Get good nutrition and sleep. Identify food sensitivities. Give yourself grace. You're worth it.

TAKE GOOD THINGS FROM TOUGH THINGS

Remember, not everything tough has to be pointless. Tough things can take things from you, but you can take things from them. Don't let something tough go by without you taking something. In 2019, I was crushing it in my speaking career and breaking personal records. Life was great until COVID-19 came. 2020 was tough. COVID took the life of my wife's grandmother. It nearly brought my career to a stop. My wife had to work overtime to compensate for my lack of income as we feared the unknown future.

That's when I decided to own it. If COVID was going to take our money and Rachel's grandmother, I would take something from COVID. Since I wasn't speaking much, I had time to spend with my wife and kids. 2020 was the worst year for us financially, but it was one of the best years for us relationally. COVID gave me time. So, I took it.

Time alone doesn't create great relationships. I know plenty of families who grew apart during 2020. The difference is how you spend the time and the attitudes you bring into the moments.

Other good things came from 2020, such as creating a nonprofit that hosts student leadership conferences. I named it "Love the Tough, Inc." I love the tough, not for what it is, but for what it makes me: tougher.

My adventure through depression took a lot from me, but I also took from it. I took a new appreciation for feeling good. I took a new-found empathy for anyone suffering. I took more grit because the tough made me tougher. I also took a powerful story to tell in my speeches. Sharing my story of depression has helped me connect with students on a deeper level.

Now, people approach me after my speeches and open up about their struggles. I've become more influential through my pain. Why? Not everyone relates to your success, but everyone relates to pain. Pain is like a chain. It can weigh us down, but it also links us together. We all relate to pain.

I'm sorry for those currently going through mental illness. This is hard. This is not your fault. Know this: You're not alone. You matter. You can find solutions. Professionals can help. Thank you for reading this book. I know it will help. Keep owning it. Beauty and meaning will come from your struggles.

BALANCE GOOD AND BAD PAIN

Our fast-paced culture can make it hard to find balance. Mental health can often be improved by balancing good and bad pain. Here are some examples of good pain and bad pain:

Good Pain: Studying, Practicing, Exercising, Talking through Feelings, Being Patient, Being Humble, Being Generous, Etc.

Bad Pain: Overactivity, Grief, Abuse, Loneliness, Bullying,

Illness, Etc.

Good pain makes gains, but bad pain drains. Good pain leads to achieving goals, deepening relationships, and creating love, joy, and pride. Bad pain will happen. It's inevitable. Take something from bad pain, such as grit or wisdom, but be sure to have people you can turn to through it all.

There are also good pleasures such as healthy entertainment, food, and recreation. Likewise, there are bad pleasures such as unhealthy diets, illegal drugs, excessive screen time, and other things that can make you sick, cause loss, or put you in jail.

The goal is to set up your life so that most moments include good pain and pleasure. Too much bad pain and bad pleasure leads to burnout, hopelessness, fatigue, anxiety, depression, and misery.

THREE MENTAL HEALTH TIPS

Beyond the common mental health tips such as having a nutritious diet, limiting screen time, exercising, and having healthy relationships, here are a few more:

1. "I See You."

Find a private room with a mirror, and take two to three minutes to make yourself feel understood and encouraged.

Empathize: Tell yourself, "I know it's hard and unfair, but I care."

Encourage: Tell yourself, "You are smarter than you realize. You are braver than you realize. You are enough. It's OK not to be OK, but you won't stay here. This is your life. People

> "Struggles are like a chain. They can weigh us down, but it also links us together. We all struggle."

care about you because you matter. Keep moving forward. I love you."

Tell yourself, "I love you," until you mean it. This felt weird, and I had to say it about 20 times. Isn't it sad that we make giving and receiving love so awkward?

Before you finish, name one thing you will do to move forward. It could be a decision to get help. It may feel weird and cheesy, but that's only because your fear doesn't want you to be vulnerable. Awkwardness can be a self-defense mechanism. Push past the awkwardness, and you'll find the real you.

2. "Breathe In. Breathe Out."

Find a quiet, private, and comfortable setting. Close your eyes and take deep, slow breaths in and out. As you breathe in, imagine positive compliments, love, and good vibes filling you. As you exhale, imagine the fear, lies, and negativity leaving you. The stronger your imagination visualizes this, the more powerful the results are. Do this for one to three minutes a day for a whole week.

3. Custom Decorating

Inauthentic environments are draining. Decorate in a way that is authentic to you and resonates with who you are and who you want to become. For example, I once had a poster of a band like Nirvana, just because they were popular, but not because I liked them. Decorate your life with quotes and role models whom you genuinely admire. Decorate it with pictures of friends and loved ones who make you smile. Keep your house and car clean and in a way that promotes peace of mind and inspiration.

CHAPTER APPLICATION:

Better Mental Health

1. On a scale from 1-10, with 10 being the best, how would you rate the quality of your mental health?

2. Who could you talk to about your mental health?

3. What have you taken from some tough moments in your past or present?

4. What are your good and bad pains?

5. Which of the "Three Mental Health Tips" is most helpful for you?

CHAPTER 8

BALANCE YOUR BUCKETS

∽

"Balance is not something you find. It's
something you create."

-Jana Kingsford (Author)

Balance makes for better mental health and a better life.
Balance doesn't come naturally because we naturally
gravitate toward whatever we desire most while neglecting
other important areas. Take ownership of creating balance so
you don't burn out or become underdeveloped in important
areas.

Imagine three buckets. Your life activities can be divided into three main categories or "buckets": people, progress,
and play. Each bucket can spill into the others, at times, or
remain separated. For example, you can do something purely for "progress," like your homework, or combine it with

"people" if you work as a team and build relationships. Still, it could be considered "play" if you find it fun to do. I'm not sure what kind of homework that would be.

People tend to overfill a particular bucket. I spend too much time in the "progress bucket." As an Enneagram Type 3, I often base my self-worth on progress and accomplishments. I risk burnout from overworking, isolating myself, and developing a lopsided sense of success. That kind of success falls flat because it lacks the other three categories. Success in all three buckets creates the best life.

Balance doesn't necessarily mean equal hours. For example, a balanced diet doesn't mean equal portions of all food categories. Find a balance that fits your personality.

THREE BUCKETS

People: Sharing moments with people who recharge you. For me, it's doing things I love with the people who love me, such as my neighbors, church friends, and family. The focus is on building relationships and making memories together.

Progress: Your goals and dreams that light you up. For me, it's writing this book. It's growing my speaking career. It's building my nonprofit. The focus is achieving a goal or task.

Play: Fun things you do purely for fun. For me, it's watching football and playing video games with my kids. The focus is on enjoyment apart from progress.

Remember, the buckets can overlap, and it's good if they occasionally do. For example, playing golf is one of my favorite activities because it fills all my buckets. I play, connect with other people on the course, and feel like I'm progressing at something. Ask yourself what's your primary motivator behind an activity you like. Progress is the main reason I play golf, and the "progress bucket" is the one I tend to overfill. I remind myself to have more fun regardless of performance (play bucket) and socialize more as I play (people bucket.)

While it's good to overlap buckets, it's also good, at times, for an activity to focus solely on one bucket. It's good to learn to work by yourself. It's good to learn how to play alone and connect with yourself by reading a novel, taking a hike, or doing something fun. Notice that I didn't mention screens. Sure, that could be an option, but more rejuvenating and fulfilling options exist. Get creative. Lastly, it's good to socialize without work or some extravagant fun activity.

Get your phone out and open your calendar. Schedule activities for buckets that need filling. Is it the progress bucket, such as house projets, daily cleaning, work projects, or other goals. Is it the people bucket, such as spending time with your friends and relatives? Is it the play bucket, such as playing outdoors, creating artwork, or having a game night? I put things in my phone calendar and then set reminders. I plan several days, weeks, or sometimes months in advance. Then, I get excited about things coming up. This is a much more proactive approach to life than just seeing what each day brings without planning. If you don't plan, you'll be like most people who settle for screen time and feel unfulfilled. Plan an array of events for the next couple of months that fill all buckets, and watch how peaceful and balanced you feel.

You can use this "balanced buckets" concept with how you decorate. Like with "custom decorating," see if your house, car, or desk reflects the three buckets. For example, does your house have something that fills the "people bucket," such as pictures of your friends and family? An inspirational poster or award could be for the "progress bucket" and something playful and fun for the "play bucket."

BUCKET METAPHORS

Here is a way to conceptualize the three buckets differently. Imagine a banana split. The banana is you. The three ice cream scoops represent the three buckets: people, progress, and play.

Now, imagine squeezing chocolate or caramel syrup on top. This symbolizes the consistent activities you must do to maintain healthy levels in each category. Have planned time on your calendar for people, especially your family. The same goes for progress and play. Schedule the activities you want to do in each category consistently.

Next, imagine toppings like sprinkles, peanuts, or whatever you like on each scoop of ice cream. These represent spontaneous and special events in each category. For example, for "people," it may be random acts of kindness to strangers, once-in-a-lifetime trips with family, and sporadic adventures with friends. For "progress," it may be attending a club or work conference or taking a school-sponsored trip. For "play," it may be a special concert, Christmas present, or travel. Variety and spontaneity keep things fresh and prevent monotonous routines.

Finally, the cherries on top are whatever extra good luck and blessings come your way. Altogether, the totality of the banana split makes for a balanced and better life.

CHAPTER APPLICATION:

Balance Your Buckets

1. Which bucket do you fill the most, and which do you fill the least? Why do you think that is?

2. How can you balance your buckets in the upcoming week?

3. Eat a banana split. :)

CHAPTER 9

OWN YOUR PERSONALITY TYPE

"Your work is to discover who you are and then with
all your heart give your light to the world."

– Jennifer Williamson (Former Oregon State Representative)

I want to finish Part One of this book by giving you the
opportunity to learn about my favorite personality assessment: The Enneagram. The Enneagram helped me accept
that people are meant to be different. We are unique, like
fingerprints. Our different personalities bring balance to the
world, but if we can't learn how to live with that diversity, it
brings conflict.

The Enneagram helped me become a healthy version of
myself rather than a toxic version. It will also help you better
understand and interact with others. Have your family and
friends take the online assessment.

According to Enneagram, there are nine personality

types. Consider which one you are most like, not which one you wish you were. Embrace your main type and understand you're a bit of all of them. Own it.

THE ENNEAGRAM PERSONALITIES

1: THE PERFECTIONIST

2: THE HELPER

3: THE ACHIEVER

4: THE INDIVIDUALIST

5: THE INVESTIGATOR

6: THE LOYALIST

7: THE ENTHUSIAST

8: THE CHALLENGER

9: THE PEACEMAKER

TYPE 1: THE PERFECTIONIST

(The Rational, Organized, Idealistic Type)

Core Fear: Being Bad / Being Wrong
Core Desire: Being Good / Being Right

- Principled, Purposeful, Self-Controlled, and Perfectionistic

- Type Ones want order and accuracy, and they enjoy rules. They fear being wrong and not doing things right.

  - When mentally healthy, they lead with high standards, strong moral compasses, and attention to detail.

  - When mentally unhealthy, they can become overly critical, rigid, hypocritical, self-righteous, and angry.

    - How to be a good friend to a Type 1: Be dependable, authentic, and consistent.

    - Possible compliment for a Type 1: "Whenever I don't know what to do, I just think, 'What would you do?'"

    - Possible career for Type 1: One that provides routine structure, loyalty, and hardworking coworkers. Ex: Surgeon, Teacher, Editor, Judge, Event Planner, Etc.

TYPE 2: THE HELPER

(The Caring, Relational Type)

Core Fear: Being Unwanted / Being Unlovable
Core Desire: Being Wanted / Being Loved

- Expressive, Generous, Thoughtful, People-Pleasing, and Possessive

- Type Twos want to be liked, and they find ways to be helpful to others to belong. They fear being unlovable.

  - When mentally healthy, they lead with compassion, service, and an awareness of people's needs.

  - When mentally unhealthy, they can become people-pleasers, overly dependent, someone who falsely flatters, and manipulative.

    - How to be a good friend to a Type 2: Say why you appreciate them and show positive support and affection.

    - Possible compliment for a Type 2: "You're such a thoughtful and caring friend."

    - Possible career for Type 2: One that provides opportunities to help, includes a supportive team, and a culture of appreciation. Ex: Nurse, Doctor, Fitness Trainer, Nonprofit Member, Etc.

TYPE 3: THE ACHIEVER

(The Success-Oriented, Pragmatic Type)

Core Fear: Being a Failure and Viewed as Incapable
Core Desire: To Succeed and Admired as Capable

- Adaptive, Excelling, Driven, and Image-Conscious

- Type Threes want to be successful and admired. They are self-conscious of how they appear. They fear failure and not being seen as valuable.

  - When mentally healthy, they lead with courage, charisma, and ambition.

  - When mentally unhealthy, they can become egotistical, selfish, deceptive, rageful, someone who exaggerates or lies to appear successful.

    - How to be a good friend to a Type 3: Give honest compliments about their achievements, competency, and positive qualities.

    - Possible compliment for a Type 3: "Geez, you make it all look so easy!"

    - Possible career for Type 3: One that provides individual achievement, opportunities for advancement, and recognition. Ex: Speaker, CEO, Entrepreneur, Etc.

TYPE 4: THE INDIVIDUALIST

(The Sensitive, Unique Type)

Core Fear: Being without Significance / Having No Value
Core Desire: Being Authentic / To Find Meaning

- Expressive, Artistic, Dramatic, Unique, Self-Absorbed, and Sensitive

- Type Fours want to be unique and to feel deep, authentic emotions. They fear they are flawed and try too hard to be different from other people.

  - When mentally healthy, they lead with creativity, passion, and emotional awareness.

  - When mentally unhealthy, they can become self-indulgent, temperamental, self-critical, depressed, and obsessed with their flaws.

    - How to be a good friend to a Type 4: Go deep with them and share your feelings, dreams, and fears. Compliment their unique qualities.

    - Possible compliment for a Type 4: "You're the most real person I know."

    - Possible career for Type 4: One offering purpose, uniqueness, and creativity. Ex: Artist, Writer, Counselor, Social Media Manager, Etc.

TYPE 5: THE INVESTIGATOR

(The Intense, Thinking Type)

Core Fear: Being Invaded / Being Overwhelmed
Core Desire: Being Competent / Being Capable

- Perceptive, Prepared, Investigative, Innovative, Secretive, and Isolated

- Type Fives want to be knowledgeable and understand things, especially data. The biggest fear of Type Five is being overwhelmed by something they can't figure out or solve.

  - When mentally healthy, they lead with focus, composure, and attention to detail.

  - When mentally unhealthy, they can become cynical, reclusive, obsessive, neglectful of others, and aggressive toward those who invade their space.

    - How to be a good friend to a Type 5: Respect their alone time and privacy. Ask for their advice.

    - Possible compliment for a Type 5: "You're the kind of person who can figure out almost anything independently."

    - Possible career for Type 5: One that challenges and increases intellect and problem-solving. Ex: Librarian, Researcher, Engineer, Etc.

TYPE 6: THE LOYALIST

(The Committed, Security-Oriented Type)

Core Fear: Being Without Support / Being Without Security

Core Desire: Being Supported / Being Secure

- Engaging, Responsible, Loyal, Prepared, Anxious, and Suspicious

- Type Sixes want to be prepared and feel physically and relationally secure. Their greatest fear is being unprepared for something terrible or left by someone they love.

  - When mentally healthy, they lead with devotion, preparedness, and dependability.

  - When mentally unhealthy, they can become anxious, feel inferior, overly dependent, panicky, and paranoid.

    - How to be a good friend to a Type 6: Help them feel secure in the friendship by vocalizing that you enjoy being with them.

    - Possible compliment for a Type 6: "Thanks for being a friend who is always there for me."

    - Possible career for Type 6: One that includes loyalty from the employer and the opportunity to solve problems. Ex: Banker, Dentist, Housekeeper, Administrative Assistant. Etc.

TYPE 7: THE ENTHUSIAST

(The Spontaneous, Fun-Loving Type)

Core Fear: Being Deprived / Being Trapped in Emotional Pain

Core Desire: Being Satisfied / Being Content

- Spontaneous, Versatile, Energetic, Free-Spirited, Distractible, and Scattered

- Type Sevens love to have fun and explore life. They fear having to struggle or living a boring life.

  - When mentally healthy, they lead enthusiastically, optimistically, and flexibly.

  - When mentally unhealthy, they can become reckless, impulsive, selfish, indulgent, and immature.

    - How to be a good friend to a Type 7: Join in on their fun-seeking adventures while balancing their energy positively.

    - Possible compliment for a Type 7: "You light up the room wherever you go."

    - Possible career for Type 7: One that offers variety, flexibility, excitement, and a fast-paced work environment. Ex: Photographer, Musician, Chef, Etc.

TYPE 8: THE CHALLENGER

(The Powerful, Dominating Type)

Core Fear: Being Controlled / Being Weak

Core Desire: Being Independent/ Being Strong

- Self-confident, Decisive, Independent, Willful, and Confrontational

- Type Eights want to be strong enough to stand up for what they believe in. They fear being powerless and not being able to control their environment.

  - When mentally healthy, they lead with assertiveness, logical decision-making, and a passion for defending the vulnerable.

  - When mentally unhealthy, they can become bitter, controlling, aggressive, dominating, and rebellious.

    - How to be a good friend to a Type 8: Be straightforward and respectful. Earn their trust and allow them to open up when they're ready.

    - Possible compliment for a Type 8: "Only a fool would try to mess with you."

    - Possible career for Type 8: One that provides

independence, challenge, and opportunities to lead. Ex: CEO, Attorney, Agent, Coach, Etc.

TYPE 9: THE PEACEMAKER

(The Easy-going, Peaceful Type

Core Fear: Being Separated / Being in Conflict with Others

Core Desire: Being at Peace / Being Harmonious

- Receptive, Reassuring, Easy-Going, Agreeable, and Complacent

- Type Nines want peace and harmony with their environment. They fear creating conflict with others by pushing their desires.

- When mentally healthy, they lead with open-mindedness, supportiveness, and calmness.

- When mentally unhealthy, they can become passive-aggressive, detached from feeling and reality, and stubborn to admit problems and seek help.

  - How to be a good friend to a Type 9: Keep a harmonious environment and avoid conflict. Encourage them to share their opinions and desires because they usually default to others.

- Possible compliment for a Type 9: "Being around you is so effortless."

- Possible career for Type 9: One that provides harmony, routine, and the opportunity to practice compassion and patience. Ex: Counselor, Teacher, Instructor, Etc.

APPLYING TO RELATIONSHIPS

I am an Enneagram Type 3 with a Wing 4 (3w4). Wings are the numbers right next to your main one. For example, if I'm a Type 3, I could have a Wing 2, Wing 3, both, or neither. Based on my results, I scored highest on Type 3, not as high on Type 4, and low on Type 2. So, I'm a 3w4. I'm a Type 3 because I strive to be successful and efficient. I have a Wing 4 because I love creating, feeling deep emotions, and being unique in what I do.

My wife is an Enneagram Type 2 with a Wing 1 (2w1). She is a Type 2 because she loves to feel needed and help others. She has a Wing 1 because she likes being organized and doing things a particular way.

Our strengths can be weaknesses. Rachel's 1 Wing can stress too much about keeping the house clean. Plus, her Type 2 is so helpful with others that she sometimes forgets self-care. As a Type 3, I can overwork. For example, my wife and kids were enjoying a summer evening sitting outside. My wife invited me, but I said, "I'm working on my book." I was letting my strength of accomplishing become a weakness in my relationships. How many beautiful nights do I have with my family? I grabbed a lawn chair. It was a better moment, and I owned it.

The Enneagram can help you understand others. You will have more friends and better friendships if you use these resources. Discovering their core desires and fears will help you learn how to connect with what they care about. Watch online Enneagram videos to learn more.

VALUES

Choose your top values from the following list and consider how different they are from the people you interact with:

- Authenticity
- Achievement
- Adventure
- Autonomy
- Balance
- Beauty
- Boldness
- Caution
- Compassion
- Courage
- Challenge
- Community
- Competency
- Connection
- Contribution
- Creativity
- Curiosity
- Determination
- Fairness
- Faith
- Friendships
- Fun
- Growth
- Happiness
- Honesty
- Humor
- Influence
- Justice
- Kindness
- Leadership
- Learning
- Loyalty
- Openness
- Optimism
- Peace
- Pleasure
- Recognition
- Respect
- Responsibility
- Security
- Self-Respect
- Service
- Spirituality
- Stability
- Trustworthiness
- Wisdom

The Enneagram Personality Test reveals values. Opposing values can cause conflict between you and others. For example, your teammate may value autonomy while you value teamwork. As a relational leader, you must meet them where they are first. You must validate their values before seeking a solution or compromise. For example, you may say, "I hear you want more autonomy on this project. First, I want you to know that I want to help you work in a way that fits you. I also care about the overall health of the team. Please explain why you want more autonomy and how it will help you and the team." This response starts by acknowledging their values and seeks to understand through additional questioning.

Continue to respond with validation and questions. For example, "I hear you say you can focus better when working by yourself. How can we make it to where you have more autonomy and we maintain collaboration?" Instead of giving pessimism to their request, give them ownership by holding them accountable for helping brainstorm the solution.

Consider having your team or family members take the Enneagram test to learn about their personalities and values. Set up a meeting to discuss each other's results. This, alone, could create more unity and understanding between you all. It may also prevent or help resolve existing misunderstandings. By understanding another person, you are better able to love them and help them.

PASSIONS

The Enneagram Personality Test reveals people's unique passions. Your passions reflect your values. For example, my passion for motivational speaking and golf includes my values of growth, achievement, and autonomy. I also value appearance, compassion, connection, courage, respect, and wisdom. One of my wife's passions is gift-giving because she values connection and serving. She also values adventure, beauty, community, justice, and security.

What are your passions, and what do they say about your values? What are your teammates' and family members' passions? How can you tap into those passions for greater connection?

CHAPTER APPLICATION:

Own Your Personality Type

1. **Personality Type:** Share your Enneagram results with a friend or family member and ask them to take the assessment. Write your values and passions and put them on your wall or your phone.

2. **Values:** Share your values with your family members or friends to learn and respect each other's differences. Consider if a misalignment of your values causes a conflict area in your life.

3. **Passions:** What are your passions, and what do they say about your values? Share with your family members or friends to understand each other more.

PART ONE SUMMARY

Relational influence starts with a healthy relationship within. Part One helps you build a better relationship with yourself. Instead of an "I'm Not Enough" and "I Can't" mentality, the "Own It" mentality encourages you to take responsibility for who you are and who you want to become. If you feel lost about your future, own it, and seek help. If you made a mistake, own it, and make it better. If you've been blessed with good fortune, own it, and help others. It's about what you do with what you have.

Take ownership of what's yours: your "marks," "mosts," "monsters," attitudes, "proud actions," mental health, and personality type. In addition, remember to balance your buckets. This is the inner foundation that a relational influence is built upon. The better you are within yourself, the better you can be for others.

In Part Two, you will learn to build better relationships with others using what you've learned from Part One. In Part Two, you will learn to connect, communicate, resolve conflict, and become a better leader.

PART 2 -

MORE THAN YOU

(Your Relationship with Others)

CHAPTER 10

BETTER RELATIONSHIPS

"To reach someone's heart, let them see yours first."

-Brandon Lee White

Relational influence starts with your inner work from Part One and ends with your "outer work" here in Part Two. It's all about your relationship with yourself and how it impacts your relationships with others. Relational influence must come from the inside out because it's difficult to sustain patience, kindness, and love with another unless it comes from an authentic internal source.

Relationships are the core of happiness and the seed of success. Healthy relationships with others are the greatest resource to humankind. When we work together, history shows that we do amazing things. Yet, there is no app for that. In an artificially intelligent world, the need isn't for knowledge; it's for genuine human connection. Intelligence can solve almost every problem, but it can't solve loneliness.

Neither can government programs or even medications for all the good they do. Humans have emotional needs that can only be fully met through other humans.

We aren't always great with relationships. We've discussed how the "bad wolf" and "Me-Monsters" scuff things up. This part of the book teaches you to be a more comfortable, confident, and caring person who can connect, resolve conflict, and lead.

Your influence on others exists in your connection with them. If you can connect emotionally with others, they will like you more. Here's a test on likability. Do people you know smile when they think of you? It's not about being good-looking or popular. It's about something more.

My neighbor, Daniel, is about five years older than me and is one of my best friends. We've known each other for many years, and I always enjoy hanging out with him. Sometimes, we play video games and billiards, do a house project, barbeque, or hang out in the backyard. We have different opinions and beliefs on things like religion, but we still get along. Daniel is one of my friends who makes me smile. How does he do it? We've all talked with someone who leaves us with a smile. Like us, they're not perfect, but we feel comfortable and happy around them. What are they doing? They are using "The 3Cs."

THE 3Cs

- Being comfortable with yourself creates comfort with others.
- Being confident in yourself creates respect from others.
- Being caring toward others creates connections with others.

> "In an artificially intelligent world, the need isn't for knowledge; it's for genuine human connection."

The first two Cs, being comfortable and confident with yourself, come from accepting your "marks," knowing your "mosts," and building confidence through "proud actions." This is what you worked on in Part One. Generally, the more comfortable you are with yourself, the more comfortable people will be with you. The third C, being caring, also comes from Part One. The more loving you are with yourself, the more loving you can be with others.

A word of caution: those with high emotional intelligence will appear naturally gifted in the 3Cs. Someone can appear comfortable, confident, or caring without truly being so. These are often charismatic people who know how to walk, talk, and gesture in all the right ways. Don't try to master techniques to fake the 3Cs. You'll lose people's trust and their friendship.

CARE ABOUT WHAT PEOPLE CARE ABOUT

How can you care about people more? Should you always do whatever they want? Nope. Should you flood them with fake compliments? Definitely not. The best way to love people is to care about what they care about. This includes what they like to do, but it also includes how they feel. If someone starts talking about a book they just read, don't quickly change the subject. Care about what they care about and talk about it. If someone is sad, don't ignore the feeling by laughing at a meme on your phone. Care about what they care about, ask questions, and listen. Better yet, use empathy and feel the emotion with them. Even if they're angry with you, care about what they care about and hear them out.

My wife likes it when I text her, "How's your day going?" She likes it when I give her massages and go on adventures around town. She also likes it when we clean the house or work in the yard together. My mom likes discussing health-related topics, and my dad likes discussing business. My brother enjoys discussing current events, traveling, and recent Marvel movies. One of my friends likes talking about sports, while the other likes talking about God. Still, another friend doesn't speak much but enjoys my company. I don't want to over-stereotype my friends and assume they only like one thing, but my advice is to learn what someone cares about and talk about it, or better yet, do it with them.

What do your friends, or the people you live with, care about? What do your siblings or cousins care about? Dale

Carnegie, author of How to Win Friends and Influence People, said, "You can win more friends in two months by becoming interested in other people than you can in two years by trying to get other people interested in you."

It's easy to focus on ourselves. We want people to want what we want, but we must remember to do the same. You don't have to like it, and you don't have to lie and say you do. You could say, "I'm not sure if I'll like it, but I'm willing to try it with you." This shows you care, and it makes them feel special. Let's be honest. Everyone wants to feel special.

ACTS OF KINDNESS

Acts of kindness are love in action, and they build connection and likability. The key is to see a need and then meet the need. This can apply to the people you live with, your friends, or even strangers. When you seek to help others, you help yourself.

RED, THE HOMELESS MAN

Several years ago, I flew to the East Coast to give a speech to a school. After getting my mid-sized rental car, I drove to my budget hotel and stopped at a convenience store. As I was about to walk into the store, I saw a homeless man standing on the other side of the street. I'm not sure what your opinion is of the homeless community, but for me personally, I don't hand out money. I know not every homeless person is a drug addict, but I've seen too many that are. Regardless, everyone deserves to be seen and loved.

Part of me wanted to help, but the other part wanted to get my snack and drink, pretend I didn't see him, and move on. That's my negativity bias. I thought, "I don't know that person. Maybe they don't need my help. I don't want to offend them. I'm busy." It's easy to talk yourself out of doing what's right.

Immediately, I noticed his tattered clothes, medium-sized beard, average height, and aging skin as I approached him. "Excuse me, my name is Brandon. What's your name?"

Without pausing, he looked me in the eyes and said, "Red."

I nodded. "Nice to meet you, Red. Sorry for being so direct, but why are you out here? Why are you homeless?"

Red looked slowly to the ground, thinking, and after a few seconds, refocused on my eyes. His voice softened, "Part bad luck. Part bad choices."

I tilted my head, thinking that was one of the most honest answers I have ever heard.

I wasn't sure what to do next until I noticed his left shoe. It had a hole in it, and his white sock was poking through. I looked over his head and saw a thrift store. I had an idea. "Red, do you want me to buy you a new pair of shoes?" Red's eyes grew wide, and so did his smile.

"Yes, please." It was the first time I saw him smile, and it was beautiful, even if a couple of teeth were missing. We walked across the street into the thrift store toward the shoes.

"What's your size?" I asked.

"11," he said humbly. Thrift store shoes usually could be better. So, I couldn't believe it when I saw a brand-new pair of size 11 sneakers.

"How about these?" I asked, holding them up.

He laughed, "Whoa! Yes, those are great." I paid $25, and we walked out to the parking lot. I watched him remove his decaying sneakers, revealing his stain-spotted socks underneath. He put on the new shoes. "Perfect fit," he said, grinning.

I put my hand on Red's shoulder and said, "Let me pray for you." After praying, I said, "I hope your life gets better."

Red looked at me with a warm smile and said, "It already has." I drove to my hotel feeling good because of this simple truth: When you help others feel good, you feel good.

You may be in doubt about whether you should help someone. Maybe it's not your place to help, but you won't know until you ask. I wonder how many better moments we've missed because we hid from our hearts.

I tried to be comfortable, confident, and caring with Red. Honestly, I was somewhat uncomfortable the whole time and wasn't confident about how things would go, but I followed my desire to care. When you lead with the heart, the hands and feet will follow.

A GOOD DEED AT THE VET

One day, I took my dog to the vet for a regular checkup. While sitting in the waiting room, I saw a lady walk in holding her cat. Tears were still wet on her cheeks, and my heart ached as I realized her cat wasn't moving. "H—H—How much do you charge for pet cremation?" She barely got the words out, unable to look the receptionist in the eye. The receptionist solemnly slowly stood and walked toward the lady and her deceased cat.

"I'm sorry for your loss," the receptionist said. "The cost is $100." The pet owner nodded her head with a muffled cry. An assistant came around and gently took her cat, which only made the pet owner cry louder. She struggled to think, slowly pulling out her wallet and handing the receptionist a credit card. After a few seconds, the receptionist said, "I'm sorry this card was declined." The pet owner searched for another card in her wallet and handed it to her. After a moment, the receptionist said again, "I'm so sorry. This one was declined, too." Somewhat embarrassed but still stricken by grief, the lady handed another card, which the receptionist said was processed successfully. The lady took the receipt, a strange exchange for perhaps 15 years of memories and friendship with an animal friend.

After the pet owner left, I knew what I wanted to do. I approached the receptionist and asked, "Can you please cancel her payment? I want to pay for the pet cremation." I was curious to know what she would say. Is that against their policy? Is the payment irreversible? The look on the receptionist's face was a mix of shock, sorrow, and gratefulness.

"Yes. Yes, we can do that. That is so nice of you." I didn't know I would be spending $100 for someone else's deceased cat that day, but it was the best part of my day. We begin to see opportunities to help when we are willing to look.

A LITTLE OLD LADY AT WALMART

I was leaving Walmart and walking to my car when I passed an elderly lady near the exit. I saw that she only had two grocery bags, but I knew even that would be hard for her to manage. She was parking the electric cart she borrowed from the store and grabbed her wooden cane. I wasn't in a particular hurry, and I was raised with some level of manners. So, I felt the responsibility to help, but I also felt anti-people feelings like, "You don't know this lady. She will be fine. Maybe you'll offend her by suggesting she can't do it." This negative anti-people talk is responsible for almost everything wrong with this world.

"Excuse me, ma'am. Can I help you?" I asked, standing beside her cart and watching her wobble

on her cane.

With a grin, she glanced at me and said, "Oh, I'll be fine." I persisted because sometimes, that's the only way kindness can win.

"Are you sure? I can carry your bags and walk you to your car."

Her grin turned into a full smile. "OK. Thanks!"

I took both bags, which probably didn't weigh more than 4 pounds, and I extended my arm as a gentleman does for a lady. We walked toward her car and talked about our local football team. She thanked me, and I said, "You're welcome," as she went on her way.

"Wow!" I thought. I literally just helped a little old lady cross the street, the classic example I heard growing up." My chest stuck out a little farther, my chin was slightly higher, and my smile was a little brighter.

A LITTLE OLD LADY AND HER TREE

About six months ago, the morning after a big

thunderstorm, I was driving through our area of the city and I saw an enormous tree that fell onto its owner's house. This tree was massive. I thought, "Man, that's a bummer! That will take a lot of time to repair and clean up."

About a week ago, my wife told me she saw a sign that said, "Firewood available for donation." It happened to be the same house whose tree fell. I needed a little firewood for the fireplace. So, I drove to that house and backed my SUV into the driveway, next to the stacked wood. A little old lady came out standing about 4'10" with white hair and a big winter coat.

I didn't need or want much wood. So, I said, "Hi! How much will $5 get me."

She said, "Oh not that much. If you give me $10, you can get more.

"Now, wait a second," I thought, "it sounds like this little old lady isn't just asking for 'donations.' She's trying to start a firewood business!" I just smiled and said, "OK, I'll take $10 worth." She was generous and gave me a little more than I needed. She told me that she is trying to raise money to pay off the cost of the tree cleanup and repairs.

Later, I thought, "That was kind of cheap of me to try to get the minimum from an old lady who needs the donations." Maybe she is a widow, and maybe she is financially strained. The more I thought about it, the more I knew I needed to go back and give her a bigger donation.

A few days later, I drove back. She came outside, and she eventually recognized me. I said, "I felt bad for not donating much to your cause. So, I want to give you $20 as an additional donation."

Her eyes lit up and she said, "Well, take more wood!"

I said, "No thanks. This is a donation."

Well, this must have broken the friend barrier, because she talked my ear off for the next 15 minutes about a lot of things. Her name is Martha, and I learned she is Mexican and was born in California in 1929. Yes, she is 96 years old as of writing this book. Her mom was Mexican, and her dad was Native American. She lived through The Great Depression as a kid and has memories of every major event in the past 100 years.

She worked at IBM in the early days of computers and read punch cards. Later, she became a secretary and a political campaign volunteer. She married and had two kids. She now has grandkids and great-grandkids, but not all of them live near her.

After listening to the sweet old lady share her stories with me while standing on her front porch, I felt a convincing feeling that I just made a friend whom I needed to keep in touch with and check in on, especially given her age. I said, "I would love to come back and introduce you to my wife."

I barely finished the sentence before she cut me off saying, "Yes, and we can have coffee! I would love that." So, my wife was moved by the whole story and came with me a couple of days later. Yesterday, in fact. We learned more about her interest in collecting angels and fine decorative plates. She loves dipping a certain Italian cookie in her coffee. So, she made sure to give us a couple to take home. She gave my wife a teapot and teacup set to take home because she doesn't use that one much.

As I sat on her couch in her quaint living room, decorated perfectly for a 96-year-old, I couldn't help but smile. I felt a warm feeling inside of connection, and it all started with a feeling of conviction to care about what she cared about. Oh, and she is planning on having dinner at our house next. :)

I'll be the first to admit that caring about others isn't

easy, and I'm not always great at it. What if you don't naturally care about what others are into or how they feel? Just do it. Like working out, when you push a weak muscle, it gets stronger. The more you choose to love, even if you don't want to, the better you get at it. After you do it, you will be glad you did.

So, who can you help this week? Who can you listen to this week? Who can you care about this week? Whether it's a coworker, family member, or stranger, find out what they care about. Look for opportunities to bring smiles to peoples' faces. You'll end up with one on your own.

PLAN SOMETHING SPECIAL

Besides looking for opportunities to help and show you care, plan something special for the people closest to you.

A SPECIAL DATE

When my wife and I were dating, I surprised her with a special date. I had a friend named Trey, who used to tour with the singer Alicia Keys. He was a genius on the saxophone and other instruments. He is now a great band director.

I took Rachel to dinner at a fancy Italian restaurant on The Country Club Plaza in Kansas City. After dinner, we saw a black stretch limousine parked on the curb. I said to Rachel, "You think we should get in?" She rolled her eyes and laughed. I said, "I'm serious. Come on."

She said, "Wait, what? What are you doing?" I reached for the door handle, and Rachel shouted, "Stop!" Rachel lunged toward me, but not before I opened the door to reveal my friend, Trey, playing the saxophone inside the limo.

"Surprise!" I shouted. Her face lit up! She felt so special. We crawled inside to find some bongos to jam on while we rode around in style.

HUMOR

Why are writers always cold? They're surrounded by drafts. :)

I'll admit it. I'm not the funniest guy you'll meet. Humor can be learned, but for the most part, you either have it or you don't. What has worked for me is learning not to take myself too seriously. Being a little goofy and even poking fun at myself is good for everyone. I think humor starts with letting go of being overly self-conscious. So, lighten up and give it a try. Just don't try too hard to be someone you're not. You don't have to be funny for people to like you.

RESPECT

There are two kinds of respect: a feeling of respect and an action of respect. You only feel respect for someone who acts in a way worthy of your respect. You might say that you admire them. However, you can behave respectfully toward someone without feeling respect for them. In other words, you don't have to feel respect to show respect. Showing respect to others, even if they don't deserve it, is a quick way to earn their respect.

Showing respect to others conveys that they matter: Their feelings, opinions, and time matters. Even if they're mean or wrong in an opinion, they still matter. So, if someone is being rude to you, respectfully reply without being rude back. If there is someone who you think is rude, be respectful and talk to them like they matter because they do. It's this self-control that helps prevent unnecessary conflict. It's this self-control that helps you maintain a positive reputation. It's this self-control that helps you help them. Use self-control by not reacting to their reaction. Instead, respond with respect.

CHAPTER APPLICATION:

Better Relationships

1. Find out what the people you live with care about. Ask caring questions. Listen. Talk about it or do it with them.

2. Find an opportunity to do something kind for someone. See a need, meet a need.

3. If you struggle with humor, try not to take yourself too seriously. Allow yourself to be goofy. Make fun of yourself in a playful way.

4. Show respect to someone whom you don't feel respect towards.

CHAPTER 11

CONNECTION TOOLS

~

"At the end of the day, people won't remember what
you said or did; they will remember how you made
them feel."

-Maya Angelou

Relational skills determine the quality of your relationships. Relationships quite possibly have the most significant influence on your future happiness. If you don't have
relational skills, you might not make the connections that
improve your life personally and professionally. Relational
skills help you turn shallow acquaintances into deep connections.

Great relationships are assets, not only for your happiness but for your career. You will advance farther, be paid
more, obtain greater job security, and find more fulfillment

with co-workers by having relational skills. If you're a manager, relational skills help you manage way more effectively because you are better able to turn other's potential into reality.

Each of the following tools carries forward the lessons previously taught in this book. You will use better attitudes and care about what people care about. While applying these tools, don't treat people like projects. These aren't literal tools like a pair of plyers to manipulate people. These are reminders and suggestions to build respect and rapport.

CONNECTION TOOL #1:

4 Steps for Better Conversations

1. Comfortable Body Language
2. Caring Questions
3. Affirming Responses
4. Selective Sharing

1. Comfortable Body Language

Body language is what you do and don't do with your face and body. I don't like to give people too many instructions on body language. I know, I've read the books on what to do and not do, but if you just try to appear to be a certain way, it's not really effective long term. Comfortable body language starts with being comfortable with yourself. Don't try to fake body language too much. It just appears so awkward and slimy. That's why the more you own your "marks," know your "mosts," and slay your "monsters," the easier it will be to have comfortable body language.

With that said, don't fidget, frown, or do other negative and distractive gestures. Have good posture. Focus on the other person by asking questions and listening instead of being insecure and thinking of yourself the whole time.

Read other people's body language to see if they're not into a conversation. If they seem sad, don't force humor to "snap them out of it." If they fidget when you hug them, give them more space. If they get excited, get excited with them. Mirroring their emotions will make them feel more comfortable.

2. Caring Questions

It's natural to talk about yourself and what you like. Resist that. Be secure enough that you don't have to make it all about yourself. Ask about others: their pets, family members, dreams, memories, opinions, hobbies, etc. It may take time for them to open up. Don't force it. Just ask caring questions. People will like you more, and you will have more friends.

I've had many conversations with people that I met at a conference. The conversation may start awkwardly, but I'm able to turn it around so that we are both smiling by the end. How? Caring questions. I often start with, "What do you like to do?" I follow up with at least three follow-up questions such as "How did you get into that? What are your goals regarding that? What advice would you give to someone interested in beginning that?" It's fun seeing people light up with joy and passion as they talk about what matters to them. This increases the connection between you two and the impact you can have on them.

3. Affirming Responses

Affirming responses make the person feel that what they said matters. Keep the focus on the feelings they're expressing. If they express sadness (not about you), affirm with, "That's so sad. I'm sorry that happened." Ask a follow-up question such as, "How are you managing through this?" If they express anger (not about you), affirm with, "That's frustrating. I'm sorry that happened." Ask a follow-up question such as, "What would you like to happen?" If they express excitement, affirm with, "That's exciting!" Ask a follow-up question about some of the details.

Affirming responses can also be encouragements and compliments, such as, "Wow! That's impressive. Interesting. That's funny. Good for you. Nice. That's cool. That's smart. You're smart. I want to do that, too." Remember, only say it if you mean it.

4. Selective Sharing

It's tempting to ask a question, hear the response, and then steal the show and talk about yourself for 20 minutes. Be selective about what you say about yourself, especially if you don't know them well. Don't be a conversation hog, and don't interrupt with, "Oh, yeah! Let me tell you a story about when I…" It's good to relate and occasionally share your opinion or tell them how you did something similar, but be selective. Less is more. Keep asking questions and learning about them. Ask caring questions and give affirming responses before you share.

JAMES, THE SIXTH-GRADE TEACHER

I was standing in an elementary gymnasium in New York doing my final preparations for my speech when I noticed a teacher standing by the stage. I may have minded my business or given a simple head nod in the past, but I've learned that connecting with people is worth it. "Hi, I'm Brandon. What's your name?"

The tall, medium-framed 55-year-old "ish" teacher smiled and said, "James."

Over the years, I've developed a sense of comfort and confidence to extend into my conversations with people naturally. With James, I comfortably and confidently started asking caring questions. I found out he was a sixth-grade teacher who used to work in the corporate world. He said he made good money, which allowed him to send his kids to college, but it wasn't very fulfilling. He became a teacher, which gave him more time with his family.

We chatted for about eight minutes about our lives. We didn't just talk about the weather or sports. We talked about our dreams and even setbacks. We connected using comfortable body language, caring questions, affirming responses, and selective sharing.

After my speech, I saw out of the corner of my eye a tall, medium-framed man bouncing in my direction like he knew me. Without warning, James, the sixth-grade teacher, hugged me. "That was amazing! Great job!" he said with a beaming smile. I thanked him and wished him the best as he left to teach his class. I was smiling, too, because that's what connecting with people does.

CONNECTION TOOL #2:

How to Craft a Compliment

1. (Person's Name), thank you for (what they did or do). It shows me that you are (character trait).

   Example: Rachel, "my wife," thank you for planning out our kids' schedules. It shows me you are caring and responsible.

2. (Person's Name), you've helped me (what they helped to achieve or become). Thank you.

   Example: Rachel, You've helped me think more about what people want. Thank you.

3. (Person's Name), I respect that you (what you respect.)

   Example: Rachel, I respect that you care about keeping a clean house.

Compliments are like Miracle Grow for relationships. Keep them sincere. Dale Carnegie also said, "Flattery is from the teeth out. Sincere appreciation is from the heart out." Avoid "compliment sandwiches" where you give two compliments with a critique in the middle. Let the compliment stand on its own. Provide compliments with no strings attached. Don't downplay the compliments. Accept them gracefully. Simply say, "Thanks. I appreciate that."

I recently joined a weekly Saturday basketball group at my church. First, let's get something straight. It's been a while since I've played semi-competitive basketball, and I ain't what I used to be! I'm the new guy with probably the most gray hair. The other players are a mix of talent, age, and height.

One of my teammate's name is Matt. He is roughly my age and a good player. Even more impressive is his sportsmanship and impact on team morale. After the game, I told him, "Hey, I like how you say, 'Good shot,' and 'Nice pass.' Then, on misses, you say, 'Good try,' and 'Stay with it.' Also, when you miss a shot, you don't get annoyed or make excuses, like I tend to do. You're a positive light on the team, and I appreciate that." That kind of specific, authentic, and purposeful compliment is much better than, "Hey, you played well."

Beyond compliments, simple words of encouragement help shape a positive culture. Instead of saying, "This isn't working," say, "Let's brainstorm ways to make this work better." You can also encourage by acknowledging the difficult thing and adding something positive. For example, "I imagine completing this project has been very challenging and stressful. Thanks for your determination and professionalism. It's inspiring." Encouragement and compliments are more powerful at motivating people than discouragement and critiques.

Don't let a day go by without complimenting and encouraging the people around you. It's the daily emotional investment into relationships that yields positive returns.

CONNECTION TOOL #3:

How to Share Your Opinion

Sharing opinions creates connections, but you won't agree on everything. Be careful not to disconnect from someone because you were careless in sharing a controversial opinion. Being mindful that not all views need to be shared, if you share a potentially contentious opinion, try it this way:

"I can see why someone would think that [opinion]. For me, I believe [opinion] because [explanation]."

Ex: "I can see why someone would think artificial intelligence (AI) development is good. It could lead to many new inventions and cures. For me, I believe that AI should be taken slowly with heavy regulations because I'm concerned about AI turning against us and destroying our world."

Ex: "I can see why someone would vote for such-and-such political party. For me, I believe (opinion) because (explanation)."

Start with a soft opener that prefaces the counter opinion to limit misunderstandings and potential conflict. Then, briefly explain your opinion with a logical and humble explanation.

CONNECTION TOOL #4:

Love Languages

In Gary Chapman's book, The 5 Love Languages, he explains that not everyone feels loved the same way. Below are the five different love languages.

1. **Words of Affirmation** – Give encouragement and compliments using your spoken or written words.

2. **Quality Time** – Give uninterrupted time to do what they want.

3. **Receiving Gifts** – Give small or large gifts. You can even create them. Just make them thoughtful.

4. **Acts of Service** – Give your time and do something for them. Say, "I'll help you with that if you want."

5. **Physical Touch** – Give appropriate physical affection they are comfortable with, such as a fist bump, high five, pat on the back, hug, etc.

Which love language do you enjoy receiving the most? Which love language do you enjoy giving the most? My top two love languages are Words of Affirmation and Physical Touch.

Think about what love languages the people in your life speak, or better yet, ask them. It's amazing how much closer you can get to someone by speaking their love language. Sit with your friends and family and talk about this page. You'll be glad you did.

CONNECTION TOOL #5:

The Emotional Bank Account

In Stephen Covey's 7 Habits of Highly Effective People, he explains the Emotional Bank Account. Whenever I compliment, use good manners, speak someone's love language, and just be a good friend, I place emotional deposits into their account. Conversely, whenever I confront someone, ask for too many favors, act too needy, give unwanted advice, or create conflict, I withdraw emotionally from their account.

Like a real bank account, you want more deposits than withdrawals. Consider someone you have a poor relationship with. Have you made any recent deposits? When you deposit with others, they want to deposit with you. As a leader, you must have sufficient funds in your teammates accounts. With your teammates, don't overly focus on tasks and efficiency and neglect the geese that lay the golden eggs. Emotionally invest into your people, and they will generate a significant return.

CONNECTION TOOL #6:

Passions and Pains

Sharing your passions, such as your interests, is a typical way to make friends. However, if you want the relationship to deepen, share your pains. Take the lead and talk about what's bothering you and what's difficult. You don't want to emotionally throw up on people, but sharing pain is a solid way to bond. When you take the lead in being constructively vulnerable, you give others permission to do the same. This creates trust and builds an environment of authenticity. This makes you more relatable and influential.

CHAPTER APPLICATION:

Connection Tools

1. Use tool #1: **4 Steps for Better Conversations** in your next conversation.

2. Use tool #2: **How to Craft a Compliment** with every person you have a relationship with.

3. Use tool #3: **How to Share your Opinion** at your next opportunity.

4. Use tool #4: **Love Languages** with each family member and share it with them.

5. Use tool #5: **The Emotional Bank Account** with each family member and share it with them.

6. Use tool #6: **Passions and Pains** with one person you want to get closer to.

CHAPTER 12

FEEDBACK

~

"Feedback is the breakfast of champions."

- Ken Blanchard (Author and Business Professional)

Feedback is food for relational growth if you have the skills to cook it and the stomach to swallow it. Helpful feedback nourishes the spirit, strengthening it for performance. Helpful feedback is not only specific and truthful but also constructive and compassionate. Conversely, harmful feedback poisons the spirit, leaving it weaker. Harmful feedback is rooted in anger, jealousy, and insensitivity, while helpful feedback comes from a source of love and wisdom. Helpful feedback is constructive, while harmful feedback is deconstructive. Relational leaders welcome and provide helpful feedback for relational growth.

Do you know what your friends and coworkers really think of you? If you could, would you want to know? If your friends took a survey about what they really thought of you, and the results were posted on this screen, would you be nervous?

That's exactly what I did.

Everything from sports, school, business, art, and capitalism, in general, is about ranking and competing. So, obviously, we worry about what people think of us. Here's the paradox. We worry about what people think of us, but we rarely do the only sensible thing: Ask.

No one has an accurate opinion of themselves. Who I think I am is skewed because I am biased toward myself, and I can't see all my blind spots. I might have a deflated view of myself, where all I see are my flaws, or I could have an inflated view of myself, where I only see my strengths. Feedback helps reveal our blindspots, but maybe we are scared to reveal them.

Humans build walls for protection. Civilizations fortify their boundaries because they don't trust those outside the wall. They are afraid of losing what little they have. In the same way, we build emotional walls of fear, insecurity, shame, and pride. We aren't open to sharing our feelings because a lowered drawbridge allows invaders access to destroy. If foreigners try knocking on the door, insisting on entry, we recoil because it's safer and easier to speak formalities from a greater emotional distance. Inevitably, they will say something hurtful. So, maybe we consider firing a warning shot before sending the cavalry. Meanwhile, those inside suffer from a lack of supplies and limited exposure to outside culture and wisdom.

Does this sound ridiculous? It is, but it's not far off from common human nature. Some people are open books, but in my experience, many are cautiously closed. In a sense, this is wise because boundaries limit outside toxicity. It can be compared to a vineyard with no fences, and outsiders come and trample the vines, destroying and gorging on the free fruit. Moreover, pests are not managed, and the plants are eaten up and wither. It's wise to have boundaries, but only if they help. For example, a tarp can be placed over the vines, but if the sunlight and rain cannot get to it, the outcome is the same: a dying plant. A relational leader protects him or herself but also understands that the free trade of feedback prospers the individual and fertilizes the soul when done properly.

THE DEFENSIVE DANCE

When I was teaching ballroom dance in college, my boss brought me into his office. With a French accent, he said, "Brandon, some rumors are going around about you. Are you aware of this?"

"Rumors? About what?" I asked defensively.

He paused, took a breath, and calmly said, "People are saying that you are arrogant, stuck-up, conceded, 'into yourself too much'."

"Who said it? Who--John, I bet John said it. It was John, wasn't it?" I snapped back.

My wall was up to myself and because of that, it was up to my boss. I wasn't willing to consider whether what they said was true. I had a wall up because I was protecting myself. But what my boss said next changed my life.

"Brandon," he said, "where there is smoke, there is fire."

That means that even if there is only a partial truth to what they are saying, part of it is probably true. Later that night I thought about what he said, and I knew there was some truth to others' opinions of me. I was too arrogant in my image and performance. Once I humbled myself and lowered my defensive wall, I became more comfortable with people's opinions. I was more open-minded and perceived others' opinions as valuable data that needed to be viewed, screened, analyzed, and applied. This led me to embrace feedback.

MY FEEDBACK EXPERIMENT

I created a survey and sent it out to some of my closest friends and asked them for their constructive, anonymous opinions of me. I created a Google Form that had five questions. Two of the questions asked my friends for positive things about me. The next two questions asked for things that I could improve on. And the last question was a wildcard for whatever else they wanted to say. I also required a minimum of twenty characters in each answer.

This is what they said...

Positive Feedback:

> 1. You help others, even strangers.

> 2. It's respectable that you seek feedback.

> 3. You do what's right even if it's uncomfortable.

Corrective Feedback:

> 1. You could listen more intently.

> 2. Don't multitask while listening

> 3. You can come off as arrogant, at times.

First, it feels good to hear positive feedback. Second, it hurts to hear corrective feedback. Plus, it's easy to dwell on the negative and give it a heavier emotional weight. By humbling myself, I noticed the trend that two people said I could be a better listener. They were right. I was willing to hear the feedback and improve. Since then, I've become a better listener. I've also worked on shifting my attention off myself and onto others to not be perceived as arrogant. I assumed the feedback about my arrogance was probably from a friend whom I haven't socialized with much since the dance studio. So, they haven't seen the progress I've made in that area. It also gave some evidence to my former dance studio boss's claim. Collectively, it was revealing without being too emotionally charged since the anonymous feedback came from people with good intentions.

What am I saying? I'm saying that we are avoiding that which we truly want: honesty. Honesty can hurt, but it also frees you. What am I suggesting? I'm suggesting we start being more lovingly honest with ourselves first, so that others can be honest with us also. Regarding your workplace, create a culture where people feel safe giving and receiving feedback. It's important for leaders and managers to not only permit feedback but also lead it. Ask for feedback randomly and periodically. Ask for people's feedback on the work culture, operations, product/service ideas, etc. Don't let it turn into toxic gossiping and complaining. Keep it constructive.

FAMILY MEETING

The same can be done in your personal life with your family members. I lead quarterly family meetings where all members give mutual feedback. There are several questions for us to answer; but first, I establish ground rules:

Ground Rules:

1. Speak honestly and with the intent to improve the relationship, not to chastise.

2. No retorts; only clarifying questions.

3. When replying to feedback, validate the feelings of the person giving feedback and summarize their feedback for clarification.

4. Any feedback can be given privately if preferred.

The Questions:

1. On a scale from 1-10, how are you? What would make it closer to ten?

2. On a scale from 1-10, how are you with your sibling? What would make it closer to ten?

3. On a scale from 1-10, how are you with your mother? What would make it closer to ten?

4. On a scale from 1-10, how are you with your

your father? What would make it closer to ten?

I pose these questions to myself first and lead by example to set the tone. I emphasize that we all want to be closer to each other, and we must be honest, as long as it's in love and not malicious.

Did you notice the question, "What would move it closer to a ten?" It's not about being a perfect ten all the time. It's about growth. This allows the person, and even requires the person, to think of what, specifically, they want to see change. If the person says something they don't like about another person, you can move to conflict resolution, or you can address it after the meeting. (Conflict resolution is addressed later in the book.) Either way, it should be addressed quickly to validate the person and improve the relationship.

The next question in the family meeting is, "What are some things you want to do intentionally as a family, as well as one-on-one with each family member? This is a good way to end the meeting on a more positive note. Then, after the meeting, we always do something fun, like watch a movie or go out to eat. This helps everyone look forward to family meetings, rather than dread them. In a professional setting, this may include providing fun snacks or a catered lunch.

How can you set up a similar feedback routine in your personal and professional life? Of course, there are programs and software that you can buy. Whichever format you choose, focus on the person in front of you. Feedback can easily become a rigid, formal, transactional process. This can create even more separation between people. A plan or process is helpful, but empathy and love must be the main ingredients for the dough to rise.

NONVERBAL FEEDBACK

In addition to verbal feedback, it's important to learn how to detect and decipher nonverbal feedback. Most people can detect if someone's facial expressions and body movements, or lack thereof, communicate disinterest, disapproval, or even disgust. Be careful not to automatically assume this is directed at you. It might be directed at you, but it also might be their default demeanor or their current mood based on someone or something else. Similarly, if someone nods their head a lot when you speak, don't assume they agree. It may be their unconscious response when listening. Instead, confirm by asking, "Do you agree with this?" or "What do you think?"

If you think someone is providing you with negative nonverbal feedback, don't address it too quickly. This may offend them or make them self-conscious. If their behavior is disruptive or disrespectful, gently ask, "I might be reading you wrong, but you seem troubled by something. Is something bothering you?" If possible, avoid public confrontation. Wait until a time when you can speak privately with the person.

FEEDBACK TIPS

Make feedback...

1. Roughly 80% positive and 20% corrective.

2. Action-based rather than feelings-based (e.g., Instead of saying, "I don't like your attitude," say, "When you rolled your eyes just now, I felt that what I said doesn't matter to you.")

3. Future solution-oriented rather than past problem-oriented (e.g., Instead of saying, "You always roll your eyes," say, "In the future, please don't roll your eyes.")

4. Timely. (sooner rather than later)

5. Empathetic. (e.g., Instead of saying, "You're so unprofessional for rolling your eyes," say, "There must be a reason you rolled your eyes. Please help me understand how you feel."

6. Especially for managers, don't just pop your head in and ask, "Hey, how's it going?" Establish time with that person to get within five feet of them and ask, "How are things going for you?" With a pen and paper or an electronic device in hand, take notes of what they said to affirm them of your empathy and understanding.

Consider these questions when giving feedback:

1. What was the good/bad action the person did, and why do I think it is such?

2. How and why was the action specifically helpful/harmful?

3. Who was affected by the action?

4. What does the action possibly reveal about the person?

5. Why do I want to see more/less of it?

6. What power do I have, or don't have, to influence the action?

7. What is my ideal outcome of this feedback, and what is my minimally acceptable outcome?

Consider these questions when receiving feedback:

1. What was the feedback given, and why?

2. What does the feedback possibly reveal about me and the person giving the feedback?

3. What did I learn from it, and what possible weakness of mine does it reveal?

4. Do I want to change any behavior as it relates to the feedback and why?

5. What power do I have, or not have, to change?

6. What is my ideal outcome of this feedback, and what is my

minimally acceptable outcome?

7. How can I affirm the person providing the feedback?

Theodore Roosevelt was correct in saying, "People don't care what you know until they know that you care." Your ability to receive and give helpful, honest feedback can dramatically improve your life because it positively affects the relationships within your life. It reinforces positive actions, diminishes negative actions, increases understanding, and builds healthier relationships. Helpful feedback takes effort, in both receiving and giving it, but you get out what you put in.

CHAPTER APPLICATION:

Feedback

1. Gather feedback from your friends and family about your blind spots.

2. Establish personal and professional routine feedback systems.

3. Establish ground rules and post feedback questions.

4. Apply feedback you receive in practical ways.

5. Remember, a healthy relationship is the goal.

CHAPTER 13

CONFLICT RESOLUTION TOOLS

∽

"A gentle answer turns away wrath, but a
harsh word stirs up anger."

- Solomon (King of Israel 970-931 BCE)

Relationships inevitably lead to conflict. We must know
how to get through conflict so that our relationships
strengthen rather than die. Many people choose either a
passive or aggressive response (fight or flight.) To be a good
friend, teammate, and leader, you must learn to manage your
emotions and to resolve conflicts.

The conflict in relationships is both the test and the
lesson. Like life, relationships will test you. The better you
resolve conflict, the less likely your relationships will shatter.
Cracks happen, but cracks don't have to lead to collapses if
they're mended. So, within each challenge is a lesson. The

conflict in relationships is the teacher of better relationships if you're willing to learn. Difficult people are the ones who teach us the most valuable lessons. They teach us to bite our tongues, be patient, seek to understand, and forgive.

Conflict can be caused by misunderstandings, abuse, neglect, disagreements, and simply the fact that we can all be difficult. Take me for example. I'll admit it: I can be too serious, egotistical, defensive, and insecure. What about you? Are you too much of a jokester? Does your sassy mouth get you into trouble? Do you gossip? Do you shut down and pout? All of this can cause conflict.

Conflict is inevitable. If you don't learn to resolve conflict, you will let one bad moment create a thousand more. One bad moment may lead to countless moments of looking back with regret and sorrow because something wasn't resolved. Consider that nearly half of marriages end in divorce, and many more remain unhappy. Why? The problem starts with conflict, but that's not the main problem. The main problem is not resolving conflict.

Think of carrots in a garden. Imagine beautiful long orange carrots like you see at the store. They look that way because they were grown right, and farmers kept all the bugs and diseases off them so that they could grow large. On the other hand, I've seen people try to grow carrots in their backyard (cough, cough, my backyard) that looked more like sick pale-yellow baby turds. Why? They probably had too much conflict. The harsh conditions of the environment, mixed with neglect, equal stunted carrots. Do you have stunted relationships with your teammates, relatives, or friends? The relationships exist, but maybe they're not what they could be or should be.

Good relationships are formed by using connection tools and resolving conflict. It takes humility, honest communication, forgiveness, and courageous action to grow through it.

Whether at home or at your workplace, don't procrastinate in resolving conflict. We acquire dings in our relationships, like hail damage on a car over time. One or two is not a big deal, but they can accumulate over time, and the relationship becomes damaged, sometimes unfixable.

There's an interesting balance we must seek to maintain while resolving conflict. You must care, but you'll be a wreck if you let every minor offense weigh you down. Take the issues seriously but not too personally. Choose your battles and avoid turning everything into something that must be discussed. Not every dispute can be resolved, but many can. Learn these resolution tools and be a better relational leader.

CONFLICT RESOLUTION TOOL #1:

Saying, "I'm Sorry."

5-Step Apology

It's a sign of maturity and love when someone knows how to apologize properly. The best way to apologize is to apologize genuinely. Not all situations require this formal 5-step process, but it doesn't hurt to use it, especially if you've really hurt someone.

> ## "The conflict in relationships is both the test and the lesson."

1. **Apologize:** Apologize sooner rather than later. If you offended the other person, they may not want to talk about it, but at least say that you're sorry and discuss more later, if necessary. A quick and heartfelt apology can be made in the presence of others, but for a longer discussion, find a private place. Take ownership. Don't say, "I'm sorry if I hurt you." That sounds insincere. Instead, say, "I'm sorry that I..."

2. **Explain:** It's not enough to say, "Sorry." Explain what you're sorry for without excuses. This shows that you understand and care. The apology shouldn't include anything they did. For example, don't say, "...but you're such an idiot, and that's why I got mad." You can discuss their part later, but make the apology stand on its own. Otherwise, it won't feel sincere.

    "...that I yelled at you."

3. **Empathize:** Say how you would feel if the same was done to you. This shows empathy.

    "I would feel (fill in the blank) if someone did that to me."

4. **Assure:** Say what you promise to do or work on. This helps rebuild trust in the relationship.

   "I won't do that again."

5. **Resolve:** The other person may need time to forgive, but the goal is to resolve the conflict and restore the relationship. Give a positive statement or question that promotes resolution.

   "Are we OK?"

   "I hope you can forgive me."

   "Is there anything else you want to say?"

CONFLICT RESOLUTION TOOL #2:

The 4-As to Calm Someone Down

GROCERY STORE THIEF

Several years ago, I was driving through the parking lot of a nearby grocery store when I noticed a male teenager sprinting out of the store with a hefty middle-aged security guard chasing him. My initial thought was, "Thief! Get him!" Did the security guard tackle him and cuff him? That could have happened if the security guard was in better shape. He quickly sputtered out about the 40-yard mark in the parking lot. Meanwhile, this teen's track coach would have clapped as he cleared the parking lot, ran across the street, and into a subdivision.

He was fast, but my car was faster. I whipped my SUV around the corner in hot pursuit. I got a glimpse of his direction through a subdivision and got lucky with a green light. He didn't know I was following him, and when I caught up, he was walking. I casually pulled up beside hom and rolled my window down.

"Hey, bud, why were you running from that cop?" He looked at me suspiciously and didn't respond. "Hey," I said, rolling at 5 MPH, "I won't get you into trouble. What's going on? What's wrong?"

He was walking quickly, and his face was full of anger, hurt, and fear. He suddenly stopped and turned toward me. "It's just so hard!" He shouted in frustration with a quivering voice.

"What's hard?" I asked gently with my car stopped in the middle of the vacant street.

He anxiously shifted his weight back and forth, looking at the ground and trying not to cry. He didn't respond, but his emotions were shaken.

"Hey, I know you're upset," I said gently, "Come here, man." He stumbled over to my window. I put my hand around his shoulder. He was covering his face. I drew him in for a side hug, and he briefly leaned into my hug, like he wanted it and needed it, but then he backed away.

I could tell he was about to leave. I pulled out one of my business cards and said, "My job is to help young people. Take my card. Reach out to me if you want to talk." He nodded his head and quickly took my card. I wanted to say more, but he turned and ran home.

I thought about him all day. Did he have good parents? Was he being abused? Will he be OK? I want to make up the ending of this story by saying that he contacted me, and I mentored him. I want to say we keep in contact to this day, and he is doing great. Unfortunately, I can't say that because he never contacted me, and I don't know how he's doing.

Some people might say I should have reported him to the police. It's important to uphold the law, but I wasn't even sure what happened. Besides, I was less concerned about the potential crime and more about the person who allegedly committed the crime. I saw someone who possibly broke the law but also a broken person. I saw someone who wanted help, but he wasn't sure how to ask for it. I saw a human needing another human, but he was scared. My point is that it's crucial to confront conflict that is within someone as well as outside of them.

It's important to realize that we can't always control what people do, but we can control how we treat them. I hope my brief moment with him made him feel that someone cares. I hope and pray he and his family are doing better.

Are you willing and capable of engaging someone and helping them calm down? Whether it's a friend, relative, coworker, or stranger, the response is the same.

The 4-As to Calm Someone Down

(Aware, Ask, Affirm, and Agree)

Aware –

Use emotional intelligence and be mindful of the situation. Is it safe or appropriate to talk to the person who is upset? Should you wait or include another person in the conversation? If you see a need to engage, move to "Ask."

Ask –

Clarify the problem and seek to understand. Ask, "Help me understand you. Are you upset because…?" Questions help you understand and show that you care. Listening helps them feel understood, which helps them calm down.

Affirm –

Affirming means supporting someone emotionally, even if you disagree. If you scold them for being upset, they won't feel understood and will probably become more upset. Show that you understand by affirming their feelings. Note that they might need some space and time before talking.

"I can see why you're upset." (why you think they're upset)

"I'm sorry that…" (what you're sorry for and why)

"I'm glad we're talking about this."

Agree –

If the conflict involves you, focus on what you both agree on and then work to resolve it.

"Do we both agree that _____?"

"From now on, can we agree to _____?"

"I agree, from now on, to _____."

There may be an underlying reason behind the conflict. For example, someone might seem upset about something, but maybe the negative feelings are being fed by something else, such as a toxic home life. If they're willing, seek to understand by asking if a bigger issue is bothering them.

Be prepared for a conflict to go unresolved. What's most important is that they feel you want to understand them. You can't always fix things for people, but you can always care enough to listen. People can choose to change, but not when you want them to. They change when they are ready to. If, for whatever reason, the problem can't be solved, be prepared to either compromise or walk away. If you compromise, you are settling for a less-than-ideal situation that may be acceptable. If it's unacceptable, you may want to remove yourself from the situation, especially if it's unsafe.

CONFLICT RESOLUTION TOOL #3:

Does this need to be said by me now?

Comedian and television personality Craig Ferguson says you should ask yourself the following question before speaking, "Does this need to be said by me now?" This could prevent unnecessary conflict. Let's break it down into three parts:

Does This Need to be Said by Me Now?

1. Does this need to be said?
2. Does it need to be said by me?

3. Does it need to be said by me now?

STAND ON YOUR MAN

My wife and I used to be close friends with a couple about our age. They were married, and she was the fun, energetic, opinionated one. He was the relaxed, easy-going one. We had lots of good memories together. One time, I invited them to my parents' lake house. Yes, the same one where my bachelor party was hosted. Apparently, conflict happens there with my friends. The four of us went on a boat ride and then anchored in a quiet cove. The weather was beautiful, and everyone was in a good mood. Well, that was about to change.

The wife started saying disrespectful things about her husband in front of us. He was there, too! In somewhat different words, she said that he was dumb and worthless. Eventually, I spoke up. I felt someone needed to stick up for him because his wife was bullying him. Like I say in my third-grade assembly speeches, "Bullying is bad." I turned to his wife and said, "Hey, I don't think it's right that you talk about your husband that way."

Let's take a multiple-choice guess. Did she apologize, cry, or go bat-poop crazy? Bat poop is correct! She said something like, "I'll talk about my husband how I want! Stay out of our business! He can stand up for himself if he wants!" Later, her husband told me to stay out of it and that he would talk to her if he wanted. I realized I couldn't force resolution even though I wanted to help.

First, some things don't need to be said at all. We get into a lot of drama, saying things that may be true but are not helpful. Second, it may need to be said, but not by you. Maybe someone closer or not as close to that person would be better. Third, you may be the person to say it, but at a different time, after both of you are calm. I like to think of it like how live TV shows are not truly live. They have a lag time if they need to bleep out cussing or cut the broadcast due to a streaker. It happens. Think of giving yourself a 3-second lag in your responses. You will say fewer regretful things.

Some people don't have the emotional capacity to talk it out maturely. If you become confrontational with them, they will probably crank up the crazy. It's better to refrain from engaging with some people.

What do you think? Should I have said anything? Should it have come from someone else or maybe at a different time? Personally, I believe I did the right thing by speaking up at that moment. We should speak up for emotionally abused people but always in a gentle way. It may not always fix it, but it's worth trying.

CONFLICT RESOLUTION TOOL #4:

4-Steps to Assert Yourself in Conflict

When you know there is something that you should say, you must say it in the right way. Here is a 4-step tool that helps you assert yourself in conflict.

1. **Opener:**

   "I want to share how I feel about something because I don't want anything bad between us." - This opener is to the point. It conveys that you're not just mad about something. You're concerned and want to help the friendship.

2. **Feeling and Description:**

   "I felt _____ when you _____." - Say how you feel (Afraid, Angry, Anxious, Disappointed, Disrespected, Embarrassed, Frustrated, Hurt, Irritated, Sad, Unheard, Unloved) and why. Make it a statement about you, not about them. For example, "I felt sad when you said I was average-looking to your friends behind my back."

3. **Request:**

   "Next time, please _____." - Ask what you want them to do. Notice the softening word "please." This softens the words that follow. Some people prefer making it a statement like, "Next time, be nice to me," but remember, you can't make them do anything.

4. **Invite:**

"What would you like to say?" - This conveys that you care about their feelings, too, and you're inviting them into the conversation.

EXAMPLE:

"I want to share my feelings about something because I don't want anything bad between us. I felt sad when you said I was average-looking to your friends behind my back. Next time, please don't say anything mean behind my back. What would you like to say?

CONFLICT RESOLUTION TOOL #5:

Dealing with Me-Monsters

1. The Exploder

They want to feel heard and respected, so give them that. It doesn't mean you have to always agree.

Empathetic Response: *Seek to understand. "What happened? When? Where? Why? How? I want to understand where you're coming from. Are you saying that...?"*

2. The Complainer

They want results but usually don't want to help create results. Listen and show respect while helping them be accountable for contributing to the solution.

Empathetic Response: *"I hear that you don't like how this person is doing this. Do you want to come with me to talk with them so we can figure this out?" "I hear that you don't like how we're doing this. What would you suggest we do differently?"*

3. The Schemer

They are sneaky, and they usually put their interests before others. Hold them accountable with a private conversation instead of a public scolding.

Empathetic Response: *Be specific. "I saw that you did/ said _____ on this particular day, and I was disappointed because it seems like you were trying to _____, and I don't think of you as that kind of person. Did I misunderstand this?" Even if they lie to you, they will respect you for how you addressed it and that might encourage them to change.*

4. The People-Pleaser

They want to be liked, they dislike conflict, and they usually lack self-esteem. These people are usually not mean. Although their actions damage relationships, they are also victims of their own doing. Let them know you like them for them and encourage them to be themselves.

Empathetic Response: *"I wanted to talk to you about something because I'm your friend. I'm worried that you aren't being yourself. I saw you say/do* _____ *and that doesn't seem like you. I just want you to know that you can always be yourself around me."*

5. The Bragger

They want to feel important. They may or may not know that they're bragging. Respond the same way as you would to a Schemer. Be careful. Only confront them if it's truly necessary because it could cause more harm than good. Regardless, always be gentle and respectful.

Empathetic Response: *"I wanted to talk to you about something because I'm your friend. I'm worried that you will come off as bragging when you say* _____. *I'm not trying to be judgmental. What do you think?"*

6. The Distancer

They don't like conflict, which is why they run from it. These people are usually not mean. Although their actions damage relationships, they are also victims of their own doing. Let them know you care and respect their privacy.

Empathetic Response: *"You don't have to talk to me if you don't want to. I'm not trying to force you. I just wanted to let you know that I care, and I don't like to see how this has such a negative effect on you. What did they say/do? What happened? If you don't want to talk, I understand, just wanted to be here for you…"*

7. The Blamer

They likely have a high sense of justice and fairness. They might believe that punishment and public shaming is more justified than reformation. They may rush to blame without ample evidence. Correct the blamer without becoming one. Don't blame and shame them.

Empathetic Response: *"Like you, I believe in accountability. We cannot promote bad behavior by ignoring it. With that said, I want to make sure our claims are warranted. Secondly, I want to help the person improve rather than simply scolded. Let's seek to understand them first, gather all information, and focus on promoting empowered solutions."*

CHAPTER APPLICATION:

Conflict Resolution Tools

1. Use tool #1: **Saying "I'm Sorry"** to someone you've of-fended.

2. Use tool #2: **4-As to Calm Someone Down** with some-one emotionally troubled.

3. Use tool #3: **"Does this need to be said by me now?"** the next time you want to confront someone.

4. Use tool #4: **4 Steps to Assert Yourself in Conflict** the next time you need to assert yourself.

5. Use tool #5: **Dealing with Me-Monsters** the next time you interact with difficult people.

CHAPTER 14

RELATIONSHIP "NOPES"

~

"Difficult people are the ones who teach us
the most valuable lessons."

- Unknown

Relationship "nopes" include being flaky, phony, shady, clingy, bossy, and other dreadful things. Do these, and people will say, "Nope." Don't be that person who everyone likes to see leave. These behaviors prevent connections, limit influence, and create conflict. Be aware of your "nopes" and be able to adjust.

1. Flaky
Flaky equals unreliable. Flaky people let others down because they aren't true to their word and don't stay when the going

gets tough.

Movie Character: Reece Bobby "Ricky's Father" (*Talladega Nights: The Ballad of Ricky Bobby*) - Reece got the itch to run away from their dinner at Applebee's just when everything was going well with his family. Turns out there's something scarier than a live cougar in a car: the fear of screwing up a good thing. Reece was afraid of commitment, so he flaked.

Common Causes: fear of deprivation, selfishness, feeling of being unworthy

2. Phony

Phony means fake. This usually means trying to be something you're not, such as seeming more cool, funny, nice, smart, or whatever. It's tempting to be phony because it seems like a quick way to fool people, but it often fails. Plus, it's exhausting.

Movie Character: Mrs. Doubtfire (*Mrs. Doubtfire*) - I hope the younger generation has seen one of my favorite movies, Mrs. Doubtfire. Robin Williams's character tries so hard to see his kids after he and his wife split that he pretends to be someone else, but it backfires. The movie has a good ending, but only after there is honesty.

Common Causes: lack of self-acceptance, fear of rejection, desire for approval

3. Shady

Like phony people, shady people pretend to be something they're not, but shadiness usually is more sinister. A shady person does something for personal gain, even if it harms another person, such as breaking promises, taking advantage of people, and gossiping. They pretend to be nice but manipulate something behind the scenes.

Movie Character: Loki (*Thor*) - Loki has the shadiest smile I've seen. He tries to play the victim but knows what he's doing. He plots against Thor for power, but he always falls short and tragically loses his brother's trust.

Common Causes: selfishness, jealousy, fear of confrontation

4. Clingy

Clingers hang on to people like leeches. A person becomes clingy because they fear loss or they over-depend on others. This can suffocate the other person. Neediness and insecurity are draining and unattractive. Being clingy doesn't add anything to relationships. Lean on others, at times, but don't squash them.

Movie Example: Dug the Dog (*Up*) - Dug, the dog, desperately wants everyone to be his friend, and he doesn't really give them a choice. The talking collar just makes it worse, but we all still love him.

Common Causes: lack of confidence, fear of abandonment, lack of emotional intelligence

5. Bossy

People are bossy because they want to control the outcome. Bossy people tend to have some anger issues. All of this adds up to their victims feeling used and disrespected.

__Movie Example:__ Cruella Deville (*101 Dalmatians*) - Cruella Deville is an example of a bossy villain who has no true friends and doesn't win in the end.

__Common Causes:__ selfishness, lack of emotional intelligence, fear of not being in control

Relationship "nopes" come from fear and an unhealthy ego. We are trying to get what we want in the wrong way. We all want a combination of autonomy and connection, but like a bully, we naturally are tempted to coerce, manipulate, abuse, and neglect. The next time you catch yourself doing a "nope," ask yourself, "Why am I acting this way? What is the core cause? What do I need to let go of?"

CHAPTER APPLICATION:

Relationship "Nopes"

1. Which "nopes" do you struggle with? How can you begin to overcome them?

2. Identify people in your life who demonstrate "nopes" and consider your response to either engage in conflict resolution or disassociation.

CHAPTER 15

MANIPULATION

∽

"It can take months to years to build trust
and only seconds to destroy it."

- Anonymous

A s you seek to connect with others, you will inevitably meet people who try to manipulate you. Manipulation is when someone tries to control another person's behavior. You might have, knowingly or unknowingly, manipulated others. People manipulate for various reasons, including getting what they want, avoiding responsibility, protecting their ego, or being raised in a toxic culture. Manipulation takes many forms. It's essential for relational leaders to detect manipulation to protect themselves and others. We will cover the following ten common forms of emotional manipulation and how to respond.

TEN FORMS OF MANIPULATION

1. Gaslighting

2. Love-Bombing

3. Triangulation

4. Projection

5. Passive-Aggressiveness

6. The Silent Treatment

7. Overcontrolling

8. Using Guilt Trips

9. Using Threats

10. Physical Abuse

1. Gaslighting

Gaslighting has become a popular term, and it means deviously making someone question their memory, feelings, identity, and sanity. The phrase "gaslighting" comes from the 1944 movie, Gaslight. In the film, a young woman has a wealthy aunt who is murdered, leaving the young woman an inheritance. Years later, she marries an older man who immediately begins to trick her into thinking she is going crazy. They have a gaslit lamp that he turns down, but when asked if he did it, he denies it and accuses her of being crazy.

Just as the woman is almost convinced that she should admit herself into the insane asylum and leave her husband her inheritance, she learns that her husband was the man who killed her wealthy aunt and is "gaslighting" her into gaining her inheritance. Gaslighting phrases can include, "That's not how it happened. This is really what happened…" or "I only did that because I was trying to help you," or "Everyone agrees with me." Again, this is said deceptively.

Movie Example: Christof (*The Truman Show*) – Christof creates a reality show in which Jim Carrey's character was born into the show, thinking it is real life. Christof unsuccessfully gaslights Jim's character into not seeking the truth.

How to Respond: Focus on what you know is true and seek outside opinions. If you know the gaslighting person's motives are devious, confront them. If they persist, disengage and distance yourself.

2. Love Bombing

You might think that a love bomb sounds like a good thing, except when it's not genuinely love. Love bombing is when someone quickly tries to gain your trust and love by excessively showing you affection, complimenting you, spending time with you, and giving you things. This person wants you to be addicted to their love. When you aren't doing what they want, they will remove their "love" to punish you until you submit.

Movie Example: Lots-O-Huggin' Bear (*Toy Story 3*) – This not-so-cuddly bear tricks everyone into thinking he is generous and kind, but when the love stops, the manipulation shows through.

How to Respond: Avoid overly relying on someone's affection for your happiness and mental wellness. Express that love should never be used as a weapon. If they persist, disengage and distance yourself.

3. Triangulation

Triangulation is when someone manipulates someone by using a third person. For example, I could pick a friend who I know will agree with me, and I say, "See, Trey also agrees that you should do my work for me. It's not just me who thinks this." Another example is, let's say I have two friends, and I ask one to sit with me because only one seat is available, but I don't ask the other. When my friend sits next to me, it establishes dominance and creates jealousy in the other friend. Triangulation uses the power of the majority to convince the minority they are wrong or need to change. The problem is it is a biased majority.

Movie Example: Regina George (*Mean Girls*) – Regina uses her influence over her other friends to control them all.

How to Respond: You probably know the correct answer without another person's opinion, but if needed, ask multiple people for their opinions for a more unbiased review. If the manipulation persists, disengage and distance yourself.

4. Projection

Projection is when someone takes what they feel and projects it onto another. For example, suppose someone consistently tells another person what to do, and the other person finally suggests something different. The first person may say, "You're being controlling." The first person is projecting their own controlling nature onto the other person. They're being hypocritical. Another example is someone cheating on their significant other but accusing the significant other of flirting with another person. People project because admitting they were wrong and taking responsibility is difficult. Instead, they shift the blame.

Movie Example: The Joker (*The Dark Knight Rises*) – The Joker tries to convince everyone through dark social experiments that no one is good when the truth is that he is simply projecting who he really is.

How to Respond: Take ownership of your actions and hold the other person accountable by focusing on the facts. Perhaps respond with, "I don't see it that way." Discuss, but don't argue. If the manipulation persists, disengage and distance yourself.

5. Passive-Aggressiveness

Passive-aggressiveness is when someone indirectly communicates disapproval. For example, a person could pout, be sarcastic, or give a backhanded compliment. A backhanded compliment is not a genuine compliment. An example is, "You're surprisingly good for a girl." Like all of these manipulations, it could be a case of naivety or tactless honesty. However, if the motive is deceptive, it is passive-aggressive. A passive-aggressive person will try to convey a pleasant and caring demeanor on the outside while harboring resentment on the inside. This kind of person wants to attack without appearing to attack.

Movie Example: Jane Nichols (*27 Dresses*) – Jane delivers a speech at Tess and George's wedding that seems loving on the surface but has some deep passive-aggressive undertones that are heard loud and clear.

How to Respond:

1. Bring the person's actions and comments to their attention as they happen.

2. Question their motives by saying, "What did you mean by that?"

3. Express how you received their comment by saying, "I took your comment to mean that..." If the manipulation persists, disengage and distance yourself.

6. The Silent Treatment

The silent treatment is a form of passive-aggressiveness that punishes someone and gains power by withholding words and affection. This method draws attention to the person using the silent treatment but in a deceptively innocent way. The person is not saying anything mean, but their intention is the same. Realize that someone being silent is not always a form of silent treatment, but if the motive is to punish, it is.

Movie Example: Hulk (*Thor: Ragnarok*) – Thor and Hulk are fighting, but when Thor says that Hulk is the "stupid Avenger," Hulk shuts down and gives the silent treatment.

Let's look at a scene that appears to be the silent treatment but is not. Elsa in Frozen is ignoring Anna, who sings "Do You Want to Build a Snowman?" Elsa is not giving the silent treatment to punish Anna. This is not manipulation.

202 | Own It

She is distancing herself to protect Anna, which is still not the best approach.

How to Respond: Address the silent treatment with questions such as, "Are you not speaking to me because you're mad? I want to talk to you about this when you're ready. Let me know when you're ready." This makes you look mature, and it makes them look immature. If the manipulation persists, disengage and distance yourself.

7. Overcontrolling

Overcontrolling is someone trying to control an excessive amount of the other person's life. They may overcontrol their schedule or decisions, such as what to wear, who to socialize with, and how to act. They may try to communicate that they know best or want the best for the other person without asking that person what they want. This sort of behavior creates an unhealthy dependency on the person overcontrolling.

Movie Example: Mother Gothel (*Tangled*) – Mother Gothel tries to control what Rapunzel does, where she goes, and even what she thinks because she wants to use Rapunzel's hair to stay young.

How to Respond: Affirm your autonomy by reminding the overcontrolling person that you can make your own decisions and prefer to do so. Otherwise, if the manipulation persists, disengage and distance yourself. If it's a parent, request to be at least part of the decision-making process.

8. Using Guilt Trips

A guilt trip makes someone feel guilty for doing or not doing something. The manipulator uses guilt to control behavior. For example, a guilt trip could be, "If you leave me, I will be depressed and maybe even suicidal." This is a difficult position because if they mean it, it is something to take seriously, or the manipulator could be lying. Another example is, "I want you to buy this for me. Don't you want me to be happy?" They may or may not be intentionally guilt-tripping, but it can still be abusive.

Movie Example: Hans (*Frozen*) – Hans had several manipulative qualities. He used a guilt trip when he falsely accused Elsa of killing Anna so that she would turn herself in. His plan literally backfired when Anna stepped between Elsa and his sword.

How to Respond: First and foremost, if they threaten physical harm to themselves, recommend professional help or even call 911, if necessary. Affirm that you understand what they want. Don't guilt them back by saying, "Well, you don't do anything for me!" If you suspect they are using a guilt trip, you can ask them, "I'm concerned that you're using a guilt trip on me. Is that what you're doing?" They will probably get defensive and accuse you of falsely accusing them. Stay calm and say, "I'm glad you're not trying to guilt trip me." If they keep guilting you, repeat those statements. Otherwise, if the manipulation persists, disengage and distance yourself.

9. Using Threats

A more direct form of manipulation is using threats. Threats are warnings that consequences will come if expectations aren't met. In the previous example of someone guilting someone not to leave because they may harm themselves, this can also be a threat. If they say, "If you don't stay, I will harm myself," it is more of a threat. Another example of a threat is blackmail, where someone threatens to divulge sensitive information about someone if they don't obey their commands.

Movie Example: Miss Trunchbull (*Matilda*) – When Bruce successfully eats the entire chocolate cake, his classmates cheer. Miss Trunchbull threatens them with having to copy the dictionary by hand and being thrown into the coal bin.

How to Respond: First and foremost, if they threaten physical harm to themselves, recommend professional help or even call 911, if necessary. In other situations, you must not negotiate with this kind of person. Say, "I do not want to be threatened. So, I must distance myself until you treat me with respect."

10. Physical Abuse

An even more direct form of manipulation is physical abuse. There is no hiding this form of abuse. It is clearly a coercive way to get someone to become submissive. It uses fear and physical power to change behavior. The person is usually older and larger, but abusive people can come in all forms.

Movie Example: Kai The Collector (*Kung Fu Panda 3*) – Besides his cool voice, Kai seeks to abuse just about everyone physically. He used physical abuse to force The Furious Five to give up their chi. He was gravely mistaken.

How to Respond: Call 911 if you are in immediate physical danger. Use self-defense, if appropriate. No one deserves physical abuse. Get help from a counselor or social worker who can help you process and cope with any emotional trauma you may have received.

CHAPTER APPLICATION:

Manipulation

1. Which types of manipulation do you use on others, if any, and how can you take ownership of them?

2. Identify people who demonstrate manipulative behavior and explain how you can effectively respond.

CHAPTER 16

FINAL LEADERSHIP THOUGHTS

∾

"People go after things, but leaders go after people."

- Brandon Lee White

Everything in this book points toward influencing others, which is leadership. What's the point of someone being emotionally balanced, strong in character, and equipped for communication if not for positively influencing others? The reward of taking ownership of yourself is not so much what you gain personally, but in the privilege of seeing the impact you can make on others. If you're like me, you want to become someone who positively impacts others. You want to be a person who helps others live better lives. When you're comfortable and confident in yourself and caring toward others, and when you have developed connection skills and conflict resolution skills, you are equipped to be what this world needs: a leader.

A leader invites others to live better lives based on how they're living theirs: purpose-filled and people-focused. A leader is not defined by age, gender, height, popularity, charisma, money, or job title. A great leader is not defined by perfection but rather by what they do in imperfect situations. A leader is known not only for what they do on the outside but, more importantly, for who they are on the inside.

Leaders are people of character. They do things right and for the right reasons. They're trustworthy and dependable. Leaders are people of competence. They learn skillsets such as the ones taught in this book and others, including delegation, adaptability, resourcefulness, etc. Finally, leaders are people of love. Nothing great can be achieved without competence and character, but it means nothing without love.

A leader is not a Marvel Superhero, but a leader does adopt the heart of a hero. Heroes help people. Many people care only about their accumulation of things. While people go after things, leaders go after people.

MY DAD

I've been blessed to have a good mother and father. They have always supported me. My father helped me to become a dreamer. He came from humble beginnings. His father was often absent, and his mother was verbally abusive. He didn't have much emotional or financial support as a child, so he always wanted to ensure his children were cared for. He went to college by his own means. He started a roofing business without anyone showing him how. He went on to do many things because he respected his potential, owned his past, and was determined to create a more positive future.

I became a motivational speaker mainly because I saw my dad doing public speaking during one of his careers. He was a role model for me to go after my dreams. That's a part of leadership: to show others that it can be done and give them the courage to try.

I can't think of many examples of how I've been a leader for my dad, but one, in particular, stands out. Several years ago, he and I discussed ideas for my speaking business in his kitchen. To paraphrase, he said I needed to be more ambitious with my career and was playing it too safe. I would agree with him to an extent, but I was offended by how he said it. I wanted him to give me more credit for how far I've come and respect the plans I had for growth. I was a little defensive, even if he was a little insensitive.

Our conversation became somewhat heated, and so I left and went to a different room. Neither of us wanted to practice compassionate communication.

I remember feeling so mad at him for not being a more caring leader in how he communicated with me. That's when it hit me. I can be a leader, too. No one is perfect, and we all need to step up at times in a relationship.

I walked back into the kitchen, sat beside him, and said, "We need to talk this out." I led a more positive conversation based on seeking to understand each other. Together, we smoothed out the conflict and learned from it as well.

Looking back, I can see how that conversation spurred me to take bigger risks and grow my business. It turned out to be a good thing for me because we resolved the conflict.

I chose to humble myself and lead a conversation that helped mend the relationship. How often do we want to shove it down, forget about it, and move on? You can only ignore the trash in a house for so long until it starts affecting everyone. Because I used conflict resolution skills, I helped strengthen my relationship with my dad.

The next time you experience conflict within your family, friends, or coworkers, breathe, humble yourself, and try leading a positive conversation. Start by asking questions, listening, and making the other person feel understood. Then, share how you feel and try to come to an agreement. If you made a mistake, quickly own it. Apologize and learn from it. Use it to strengthen the relationship, not weaken it. You have power to improve the relationships in your life and the environments you live in. Even if you're not the manager, you can positively influence your environment through relationship.

THE PRIORITIES OF A LEADER

People go after things, but leaders go after people. Leaders prioritize relationships. Former President Dwight D. Eisenhower was the Supreme Commander in World War 2, and he was known for his ability to prioritize. Below is the "Eisenhower Box." A leader's priority should be in the top two "important" boxes.

	URGENT	NOT URGENT
IMPORTANT	DEAL WITH 1. Impending Deadlines 2. Mental/Physical Health Crisis 3. Reporting Abuse	DO MORE OF 1. Meaningful Family/ Friend Time 2. Goal Setting/Organizing 3. Self-Care
NOT IMPORTANT	DELEGATE/DIMINISH 1. Spam Calls 2. Unnecessary News/ Sports/Gaming 3. Unnecessary Phone Notifications	DELETE 1. Spam Emails 2. Unnecessary Scrolling 3. Celebrity Gossip

> "A leader invites others to live better lives based on how they're living theirs: purpose-filled and people-focused."

not always urgent, but it's always important. Being in person is best, but you can grow relationships virtually if necessary. Group time is good, but plan one-on-one time also. Discuss things you can do together. Each event doesn't have to be big. It can be as simple as having a short conversation and learning more about their interests and struggles.

Based on the example below, create a relational goal that is centered around an activity they enjoy. Take the lead and grow relationships because that's what's important.

Person: Dave (Teammate)
I want to: have lunch and learn more about him and encourage him
Before: the end of this week
Because: I want to strengthen our relationship.

Person: Tom (Teammate)

I want to: go golfing and learn more about him and encourage him

Before: the end of this week
Because: I want to strengthen our relationship.

Person: Brad (Teammate)

I want to: play chess and learn more about him and encourage him

Before: the end of this week
Because: I want to strengthen our relationship.

HONOR YOUR LEADERS

We have leaders who influence us in various ways, shaping us into who we are. Their influence stays with us like sand in our shoes long after we leave the beach. My father influenced me to take positive risks. My mother influenced me to proceed with wise caution. My brother influenced me to always remember to have fun. My wife influenced me to stay humble. All these relationships have made me better.

MR. WILKINS

My middle school social studies teacher and cross-country coach was Mr. Wilkins. He was a friendly but no-nonsense former army guy with a buzz haircut and professionally dressed attire. He commanded his classroom with authority. Misbehavior was quickly addressed, but he was fair. Everyone respected him.

Mr. Wilkins was in his thirties but could run like us teenagers. I always wanted to impress, so I ran extra hard when he was around. Mr. Wilkins would often lead us in our practice and sing cadences from

his army days, "I don't know, but I've been told! You never slow down; you never grow old!" Yes, that is a direct line from Tom Petty's song about Mary Jane.

I moved away after my eighth-grade year and many years passed. After I graduated college, I discovered that Mr. Wilkins was now teaching in a district near me. At first, I was a little intimidated to reach out, but I decided to do it anyway and invite him to coffee. When we reconnected, I was pleased to find he was the same person I remembered. We enjoyed catching up and even went on a run together a few days later. I wasn't running consistently like he was, and it took everything in me to keep up and not seem like I was dying.

More years passed, and when I reconnected with him, I learned that he has Parkinson's disease, which is a brain disorder that causes unintended movements, such as shaking, stiffness, and difficulty with balance and coordination. Mr. Wilkins was taking medication to prevent the shaking, but it was apparent that the person sitting across the table was a different person than I had seen a couple of years ago. He couldn't run like he used to. So, we went on a gentle walk. His memory occasionally slipped, and sometimes, he needed a few extra seconds to find the right words. You know the phrase, "Never meet your heroes because they may turn out not to be so heroic?" It's true; I saw a man I once respected for his physical strength who now suddenly seems not so heroic. But I also saw someone better take his place. I saw Coach Wilkins become softer, kinder, and more patient. How he responds to Parkinson's teaches me how to respond to life.

I realized that what I truly respected most about Coach wasn't his physical abilities. It was his leadership abilities. His people skills to connect, inspire, and push people beyond their limits. He is one of the leaders I liked. He is one of the leaders who inspired me to action. How? Relational leadership.

When you read this, Mr. Wilkins, I want you to know that you are one of the leaders who helped me build a better life while I was young. You helped me own it. I look forward to our next meeting and pray for the best for you and your family and your future.

As I write this chapter, I had coffee with Mr. Wilkins this morning. He's comfortable, confident, and caring even through his struggles. He showed me how to run through physical pain, and now he's showing me how to grow old through life's pains. He's still leading. When you get older, reconnect with an adult who was a leader in your life. Keep the relationship going.

Leaders don't push people into better futures. They invite them. They encourage them, and they model the way. Who has nudged you into a better future? Tell that person what they mean to you.

Dale Carnegie, author of the classic self-help book How to Win Friends and Influence People, gave the leadership advice to "Give people a fine reputation to live up to, and they will make prodigious efforts..." In other words, if you treat someone like a child, they are more likely to act like a child. If you treat someone like they're dumb, they're more likely to believe it and be dumb. Conversely, if you treat someone as kind, respectable, intelligent, and important, they are more likely to act that way. Notice, it's not just about you being friendly and respectful to them, but it's also about conveying to them that they are those things, too. You don't have to lie, but if you see past their outer flaws, you may see more on the inside.

Leaders remind people of who they truly are. They help others own their "marks," "mosts," and "monsters," choose "proud actions" and positive attitudes, connect with others, resolve conflict, and become leaders. These are the things needed in your home and workplace, and they are all within your power. Regardless of your title or age, unlock the power of your influence. Now is the moment. It's time to own it.

CHAPTER APPLICATION:

Final Leadership Thoughts

1. Apply the relational skills you've learned in this book toward a relational goal. Pick a few people to grow your influence with.

2. Honor a leader in your life by writing, calling, or having an in-person conversation about your appreciation for their influence in your life.

PART TWO SUMMARY

Relational influence requires connection and the ability to maintain that connection through communication skills. You've learned the skills and have acquired the knowledge to help you resolve conflict and lead others from the inside out.

With the "Own It Mentality" and strategies, you will have better relationships at work and at home. Refer to this book for reminders on how to take ownership of what matters most. I want you to know that you can be everything in this book and more. You are what the world needs. Own it.

Psst... read the next page. (The Afterword)

AFTERWORD

"I'll try it." I said, shrugging at the barista as he pointed to a new latte on their menu.

My wife stood in a corner of the room with dark bookshelves and couches. The coffee house was half full, with people of various ages talking, reading, and working on laptops.

"It will be right out," the college-aged barista said with a warm smile. Grabbing my coat, I strolled over to Rachel, who was glancing through a Christian book.

"I like this place," I said to her while studying the plethora of old and new books. "You know what…" I started in on a thought but quickly paused.

"Yeeees?" Rachel urged the rest out. She knows me too well.

"I want to write a really good book." I shifted my weight and became more confident in my tone. "You know, one that makes them say, 'This really helped me.'"

"But you've already written a few books." She said in between flipping pages.

"Yeeeees… but…" I paused and sat next to her on a brown suede sofa. "I'm a better writer now." I think I said that more for my sake than hers.

Sensing my passion, Rachel looked up from her book. "Well, do it, then," she said with an ornery grin.

"Midas Golden Latte!" The barista shouted from behind the counter. I hopped up to retrieve my prize and returned to my warm spot on the sofa.

A beautiful rustic clay coffee mug sat before me, with steam rising gently into the air, inviting me in.

"I'll try it," my wife said, nodding to my latte. I handed her my mug and stared at the bookshelf. "Mmm! It's good!" She exclaimed wide-eyed.

"Yeah, me too..." I murmured with a dream set into motion and growing in my heart. "I'll try it."

~

Since that March day at Overflow Coffee House in Liberty, MO, I spent nearly every day for a year writing the original version of this book, Own It: The Mentality for Building a Better Life While You're Still Young. Then, I revised it for an older audience, which is the edition you are reading now.

My wife and family have been supportive during the countless hours I spent trying to create something worthy of reading. Shoutout to my friends who listened to my ideas for the book and brainstormed with me. I'm blessed to have good relationships.

So, if you find yourself visiting Overflow Coffee House,

order a Midas Golden Latte and make your way back to the bookshelves. If you look hard enough, you might find a special copy waiting for you.

ABOUT THE AUTHOR

Author and speaker, Brandon Lee White has spoken to roughly one million people about taking ownership of their lives. He has been featured on TEDx, TLC, Discovery Health, FitTV, and even Wheel of Fortune.

He attended Rockhurst University, earning his Master's in Business and a double major in Business and Psychology.

He is the founder and president of Love the Tough, a nonprofit providing leadership conferences.

Brandon loves spending time with his beautiful wife and wild children at home. They enjoy leading and serving in their church. Plus, Brandon can't get enough of barbecuing, golf, hunting, chess, and meeting new people as he travels around the country.

For speaking engagements, please visit www.BrandonLeeWhite.com.

Website: www.brandonleewhite.com
Nonprofit Website: www.lovethetough.com
Email: Brandon@brandonleewhite.com
Social Media: @Youthmover
YouTube: @Youthmover

www.ingramcontent.com/pod-product-compliance
Lightning Source LLC
LaVergne TN
LVHW051400080426
835508LV00022B/2913